YOUR STORY ISN'T OVER YET

"*Your Story Isn't Over Yet* is a powerful and important book. Grace's story is filled with pain, tragedy, and loss; but in the end, it is a story of grace, hope, and triumph. Grace has told her story in a vulnerable, transparent, and engaging way that draws in the reader and gives all glory to God. Once you start reading this book, you won't want to put it down. Grace's life story is a testament to God's loving kindness and faithfulness and is evidence that there is no life beyond His restoring power. I pray that many will read this book and be inspired not to give up no matter what they are going through."

Joshua West
Pastor, Author, and
Executive Director of World Challenge Inc.

A Breathtaking, Transforming Story
to Encourage Your Soul in Times of Darkness

YOUR STORY ISN'T OVER YET

A Memoir

Grace Valentine Gagnon

AMBASSADOR INTERNATIONAL
GREENVILLE, SOUTH CAROLINA & BELFAST, NORTHERN IRELAND
www.ambassador-international.com

Your Story Isn't Over Yet
©2025 by Grace Valentine Gagnon
All rights reserved

ISBN: 978-1-64960-793-5, hardcover
ISBN: 978-1-64960-617-4, paperback
eISBN: 978-1-64960-668-6

Cover Design by Hannah Linder Designs
Interior Typesetting by Dentelle Design
Edited by Kimberly Davis

No part of this publication may be reproduced, distributed, or transmitted in any form or by any means, including photocopying, recording, or other electronic or mechanical methods, without the prior written permission of the publisher, except in the case of brief quotations embodied in critical reviews and certain other noncommercial uses permitted by copyright law. For permission requests, contact the publisher using the information below.

Unless otherwise noted, Scripture quotations taken from the New Living Translation (NLT) of the Holy Bible, New Living Translation, copyright © 1996, 2004, 2015 by Tyndale House Foundation. Used by permission of Tyndale House Publishers, Inc., Carol Stream, Illinois 60188. All rights reserved.

Scripture marked KJV taken from the King James Version of the Bible. Public Domain.

Ambassador International titles may be purchased in bulk for education, business, fundraising, or sales promotional use. For information, please email sales@emeraldhouse.com.

AMBASSADOR INTERNATIONAL
Emerald House
411 University Ridge, Suite B14
Greenville, SC 29601
United States
www.ambassador-international.com

AMBASSADOR BOOKS
The Mount
2 Woodstock Link
Belfast, BT6 8DD
Northern Ireland, United Kingdom
www.ambassadormedia.co.uk

The colophon is a trademark of Ambassador, a Christian publishing company.

Table of Contents

Foreword   3

Disclaimer   7

1
Façade: Hiding the Authentic Me   9

2
Origin: Family and Faith   15

3
Willing Vessel: God's Love for Humanity   19

4
Unexpected: Alone and Afraid   23

5
Dilemma: Please Don't Take My Baby   33

6
Preyed Upon: Make Your Stand, Grace   41

7
Divorce 1: Defiled and Broken   63

8
DXB: High Up in the Sky   77

9
Divorce 2: Disappointed but Determined   89

10
Mon Québécois: Coup de Foudre   111

Bibliography   135
About the Author   137

Dedication

I am thankful for God's abounding grace, favor, mercy, and strength. Jesus is my first Love, and this book would not have been possible without Him. I am grateful that He orchestrates my life and directs my steps. He is the main reason I live, love, sing, and write.

May every person reading my story find hope, clarity, forgiveness, courage, healing, and breakthrough. May dysfunctional patterns, unhealthy cycles, and generational curses be broken. May you be the change you wish to see. I pray for blessings and victory upon all the generations that come through you. Your story isn't over yet! God can turn it around.

Thank you, Mom and Dad, for raising and guiding me. Thank you for all the sacrifices you have made over the years. I love and appreciate you. I know you did the best you could with what you had. My life would be incomplete without you. I love you so much.

To the rest of my dear family, relatives, and close friends, thank you for being there for me when I needed you. Thank you for adding color and beauty to my world.

Thanks to the people who supported me in this journey of writing through encouragement, advice, and prayer.

To those I have hurt in the past due to my own inner struggles, I am truly sorry. I never meant to cause you pain.

To those I have inspired, I am glad to somehow be a tiny part of your journey. Be blessed, be a blessing, and keep moving forward.

To my beloved husband Joel, my soulmate, best friend, and the love of my life, I am grateful for you. Your love, support, calmness, and understanding have impacted my life tremendously. You make my world a better place. You have, indeed, brought me so much security and stability. Thank you for daily motivating me to write. You are an amazing husband and father. I love you deeply. You are my dream come true and the answer to my prayers.

And now, a very special dedication to my little girl, my precious daughter, Rania: you are God's incredible gift to me. You have brought so much meaning to my life, and I love being your mommy. You will read this book one day when you are much older. I know that it will bring about so many different emotions and questions; but I pray that my life experiences will remind you of how strong, resilient, and versatile women are. May my life always direct you to the amazing love of God. He will never fail you. I am so proud of you, Rania, and I love you forever!

Foreword

In *Your Story Isn't Over Yet*, a deeply personal revelation, Grace Valentine Gagnon takes us on a compelling journey. This is an honest—at times, gut-wrenching—memoir that showcases the remarkable power of faith, resilience, and redemption in even the darkest hours of a young woman's life. As you delve into the pages that chronicle her journey, you will be inspired by her courage to confront the horrible abuse she suffered through so much of her life at the hands of what could only be called toxic, vile predators. With each turn of the page, you're drawn into her world, feeling her pain, sharing her agony, and shedding her tears.

The chapters entitled "Unexpected," "Preyed Upon," "Divorce 1," and "Divorce 2" document Grace's experience of being raped, physically and sexually abused, and molested as a vulnerable teenager. These chapters show firsthand the awful things that can happen when the most vulnerable among us, women and children, are considered unimportant. But this vulnerable young woman refuses to let her story end in despair and bitterness. In Grace's own words, "I may not fully understand (now or ever) why certain things happened. However, I do know that He will work things out for my good as He always has. I have learned to trust in His faithfulness. Through every hardship, I remind myself that my story isn't over yet."

What sets this book apart is not only the tale of survival but the way it demonstrates Grace's determination to find her wings and fly again, both literally and metaphorically. Her incredible journey of becoming a flight attendant for the prestigious Emirates Airlines, documented in the chapter entitled "DXB: High Up in The Sky," leaves us truly marveling at Grace's resilience. Despite just surviving an abusive marriage and divorce, she boldly enters a hotel ballroom, surrounded by around three hundred other applicants in elegant attire and hair immaculately styled. In the way only she can, Grace describes how she felt entering that beautiful ballroom: "Flabbergasted. Yup, that is how I was feeling. Extremely flabbergasted, uncomfortable, and awkward. I was the only one underdressed!" She might have been lacking in elegant attire; but she was full of faith, hope, and love—and that proved to be more than enough. Her strength, her compassion, and her smile radiated the warmth and acceptance that Emirates was looking for. And so, from the deepest valleys of humiliation, Grace emerged not around her pain and brokenness but through it, and high up in the sky she soared.

As the book ends, we are treated to a story of unexpected love that reads like a romance novel come to life. Grace's encounter with a handsome Canadian firefighter, their *coup de foudre*, their magnetic connection, their phone calls, text messages, and letters sent across oceans and continents all eventually led to them promising their love and devotion to one another in the bonds of holy matrimony. Their love story took an even more beautiful turn when Joel embraced the role of father to Grace's lovely daughter, Rania. It's like he was the puzzle piece that had always been missing.

It is my prayer that through Grace's book you will know that God can take what others meant for evil and turn it to good; that God can take what you thought were lost ravaged years and restore them to you as gentleness, wisdom, and compassion; that you will realize that no matter how deep your wounds, how profound the pain, your story isn't over yet. God will come through for you!

Chad Burton

Senior Pastor, Living Word Global Church

Chaplain, Irving Police Department

Disclaimer

This work depicts actual events in my life as truthfully as recollection permits. Everything in this memoir is true; it is my life story. As a gesture of goodwill toward the families, I have removed names of people mentioned.

The purpose of this memoir is not to hurt, destroy, or tear down anyone. I believe that people can make the choice to repent, change, grow, make amends, and move forward. No one is out of God's reach, and nothing is hidden from Him. I forgive everyone who has hurt me. I sincerely hope they will be better people and turn their lives around with God's help.

I have no intention of reaching out to my abusers or former intimate partners; I release them to God. Forgiveness does not always require reconnecting with the people who abused or hurt you. Wisdom, discernment, and discretion are necessary.

The safety, well-being, and peace of my family are of utmost priority to me. My parents are mentioned quite often in this memoir. I love and cherish them. This book is not intended to dishonor them.

I share my authentic, raw experiences in order to be honest and open with my readers. The purpose of this memoir is to help other individuals and families find healing. It is meant to spread hope and courage. It is meant to direct you to the One greater than I: Jesus.

1
Façade: Hiding the Authentic Me

Hope. Laura Hope. That is what I told myself I would name my unborn child. I became pregnant at the age of seventeen in Africa and, for some strange reason, felt strongly in my heart that it was a baby girl. Despite my fear and uncertainty about what was to come, I wanted to keep the baby and protect her, my Laura Hope.

I had been a virgin—innocent and ignorant about love, sex, relationships, and pregnancy—a teenager with a flair for words who loved God, her family, and people. Always smiling, singing, and helping others, I wanted to make a difference in this world, to touch lives and spread hope. Now I felt cut off from the rest of the world, lonely, lost, afraid, and ashamed.

I grew up in a caring family that operated under the strict control and harsh discipline of an overprotective, closed-minded father. He was a responsible man who was always there when we needed help and worked hard to provide for us. I love, appreciate, and respect him; and I know he loved my siblings and me in his own way. Our relationship has improved over the years, and he has made positive changes in his life; however, the fear, anger, and anxiety that result from his own past wounds and unresolved issues infused his parenting and created an atmosphere in our home that affected me significantly.

Insecurity and pride caused him to worry about what people might think; so he dictated what I should wear, whom I should talk to, where I should go, what I should say, and how I should feel and behave. Controlling and unreasonably strict, he often thought about worst-case scenarios and wanted to manage everything, needing people to respect him and be in awe of what a proper family we were. His suspicious, authoritarian nature brought fear and panic into my life.

I could never be my true self, and neither was I free to express myself. My father did not like it when I cried and said I was too emotional. He always told me to be strong yet did not allow me to have the independence or freedom I needed. He sometimes drove to my school to see if I had played truant, but I was never that girl; I was sensible, polite, honest, kind, and well-behaved. Nonetheless, his irrational fears made him doubt me.

My teenage years were unpleasant. I rarely had friends outside of school and was always closely supervised because I was female. Once when I was about thirteen, a boy from school called with a homework question. When he realized he had reached the wrong Grace's house (our class had two), he apologized and hung up. Infuriated, my father hit me, even after I explained the misunderstanding and assured him that I had done nothing wrong. It was just one of many similar incidents.

Fear and uncertainty back then prevented my mom from interfering with his methods, and I wish she could have put an end to all the terrible beatings I endured. Maybe she did try; maybe she did not try hard enough. She could have been afraid, helpless, or unsure of what to do. Perhaps she prayed and believed my father would change. Her tolerance, silence, and lack of action may have enabled my father. In any event, her character and mindset are different now: she is stronger, wiser, bolder, empowered, and independent. They remain happily married and look for better ways to show us that they love us.

No excuse exists for violence, abuse, or harsh discipline; but I have learned to forgive and love my father. Reflecting on my life and making changes to focus on being a better mom and to grow deeper in my relationship with God helped me understand his humanity: the struggles, challenges, mistakes, and fears he faced as a man who experienced chaos and dysfunction while growing up and served in the army for over twenty years.

Now as an adult, wife, and mother, I understand that no one parents perfectly. We try to raise our kids to the best of our abilities and do what is right for them. Every situation is different; various factors can cause stress or overwhelm us. The key is to not lose determination: keep trying and get help if necessary. Ask God for wisdom and strength. Practice self-care. Breathe.

I still face frustration and tension sometimes, especially around my dad. Sometimes, I feel uncomfortable being alone with him. Spending time with God helps, and I check my heart often to ensure that unforgiveness and bitterness have not crept in silently. I look for ways to show kindness and enjoy watching him bond with my daughter and husband.

I made peace with my past and released the burden to God. When it weighs me down again, I turn to Him and focus on the present and the positive. I love my parents and chose to forgive them, counting my blessings, practicing intentional gratitude, and reminding myself of their good qualities.

God will transform each of our lives in His perfect timing to reveal areas we need to repent from. If we choose not to make those changes, we are accountable to Him. I, therefore, want to focus on my own journey—improvements I can make, patterns I can change, cycles I can break, and things I can be responsible for.

I do not share these things to tear down my father or to paint a bad picture of my mother. I care about them deeply and now have a good relationship with them. We may not always see eye to eye, but I still love and respect them. Rather, this introduction of my early years is intended to help you understand the effect of certain events, even later in life, as some of the repercussions linger. Worrisome patterns, behaviors, emotions, random tics, strange compulsions, and unhealthy thoughts still present themselves. Sleep paralysis and nightmares were the norm for quite a long time. Not all of these long-term effects were caused by events of my childhood; some resulted from abuse that happened later in life, bringing about anger, numbness, insecurities, worry, sadness, and anxiety.

Everyone wages inner battles, big or small, even if they are not visible to others or spoken of openly; but no one has to remain stuck in a given situation. Take the first step toward the right direction. God is with you and will not turn His back on you. Do not give up or lose faith. Welcome Jesus into your life and decision-making and surround yourself with supportive, understanding, loving friends and family members who want the best for you. Get involved in a good church community. Do not isolate yourself. Things will get better when you reach out and open up.

The comedienne Gracie Allen is reported to have said, "Never place a period where God has placed a comma."[1] My optimistic character plays a role in my strength and resilience, but without Jesus in my life, I would be utterly lost and destroyed. His love, favor, protection, mercy, and guidance carry me through the storms of life. His Divine presence and mighty hand have been upon me from my earliest days. I may not fully understand (now or ever) why certain things happened; however, I know He will work things out for my good as He always has. I have learned to trust in His faithfulness. Through every hardship, I remind myself that my story isn't over yet!

Genesis 50:20 says, "'You intended to harm me, but God intended it all for good. He brought me to this position so I could save the lives of many people.'" I can relate to the story of Joseph. In fact, when I was a young teen at church camp, the speaker paused during a session and looked out at the crowd as though she were searching for someone. After a moment, the room went silent; and it felt awkward when she locked eyes with me intently while everyone else turned to see what was happening. She said she had a word from God for me specifically: that I was the female version of Joseph. She also mentioned that I would face many "red tapes" in life, but God would get me through everything and be with me.

---

[1] "Gracie Allen Quotes," AZ Quotes. https://www.azquotes.com/author/265-Gracie_Allen, Accessed June 27, 2024.

I realized that finding closure or getting answers is not always necessary; neither will I always get the apology I want. If anyone can transform a person fully, it is God. He has been working in my dad's life all these years through the struggles. Releasing this area of my life to God has brought peace, self-awareness, healing, humility, blessings, growth, and restoration. It has also enabled me to be more compassionate toward myself, as I am my own harshest critique.

You are probably wondering what happened to Laura Hope. Please keep reading with an open mind and a receptive heart.

2
Origin: Family and Faith

I am Singaporean, as are my parents and grandparents. Our ancestors came from India. English is my first language. Singapore's four major races—the Chinese, Malays, Indians, and Eurasians—contribute to its multicultural heritage, diversity, delicious food, and freedom of worship. English is the major form of communication in Singapore and the language of instruction in our schools; but we learn other languages as well, such as Mandarin, Malay, or Tamil.

As I write this chapter, my parents will be celebrating their forty-second wedding anniversary in just a few months. They fell in love and married when my dad was twenty-one, my mom eighteen. I pray that God will extend the days of their lives.

My elder brother, their firstborn, arrived in 1981. A second son was born in 1982 and died from complications a week later. When they welcomed me on October 8, 1983, doctors diagnosed severe pneumonia and told my parents to be prepared for the worst. They were devastated by the thought that they might lose me, too. My mom's elder sister came to visit and told them about Jesus' love, power, and goodness, explaining that only God has the power to give or take life. As she continued to share, my parents felt hope, faith, and comfort enter their broken hearts. My aunt and some members of her church came to Toa Payoh Hospital to pray for me.

The next day, the same doctor who said I might not survive told my parents I was completely fine and could soon be discharged from the hospital. That day, my parents believed and gave their hearts to Jesus. They knew that it was a miracle. It was probably their first known encounter with God; and they experienced His love, power, and healing. Although they originally planned to call me Lavanya, my name became Grace, so I would always remember I am alive by the grace of God.

God's faithfulness, favor, and mercy have never left us. Through every situation, He has always remained true. Nine years later, my parents had another son, making us a family of three children. We are all married now. My parents currently have three grandchildren and love being grandparents.

Like any of us, my parents have their strengths and weaknesses, too; nonetheless, they persevere through every hurdle in life. My father is a strong, simple, brave, genuine man. He embraced different opportunities—including full-time ministry—after spending more than twenty years in the army, and he loves to find ways to lend a helping hand. Street-smart and resourceful, he is generous, committed, and good at fixing things. His favorite movies feature action, war, and kung fu. He loves eating together as a family, trying different types of cuisines; and he does his best to be there when we need him.

My mother is smart, patient, prayerful, diligent, and creative. She is an excellent cook and homemaker, as well as a dedicated early childhood educator who displays professionalism, gentleness, and compassion with her young students. She cares about the family and still checks on me regularly, though I now live in Canada. An efficient, hard-working woman, she is also financially generous, not only toward the family but also to those in need and to the Kingdom of God, even though she is not wealthy and has needs of her own. She is grateful for all that God has done for her and therefore wants to be a channel of His blessing to others.

I lived two years in Uganda, seven years in Dubai, and have now settled in Montreal with my amazing husband, Joel, who is French Canadian. Singapore, with its rich culture and tropical weather, will always be the homeland close to my heart; but I have learned to embrace the four seasons in Canada.

Joel loves spending time with my parents. He enjoys talking to them and hearing about their life experiences, and they get along very well. What a blessing it is to have a husband who cares about my parents! I do the same with my mother-in-law, showing her love and checking on her often. Joel and I respect and cherish our parents, and we try to set the right example for our daughter, Rania, who adds so much affection, laughter, and meaning to our precious little family. God is good!

There is no perfect parent. Some struggle; some try their best; some make more mistakes than the rest. Some raise children based on what they were exposed to. Some fail or are naturally great at parenting; and some never give up, despite the challenges life throws at them. Love, patience, forgiveness, mercy, gratitude, trust, and communication are so vital in parenting and relationships. Praying together helps keep the bond strong. When God is at the center, everything flourishes.

I am tremendously thankful for all that we have and blessed to be Rania's mommy and Joel's wife. As a family, we are learning to be grateful, forgiving, and united. Falling in love with my husband has made me realize that he is home for me. Home is wherever he is. "Sometimes home isn't four walls. It's two eyes and a heartbeat."[2]

---

[2] "Quotes 'nd Notes," https://quotesndnotes.tumblr.com/post/182484246946/sometimes-home-isnt-4-walls-its-2-eyes-and-a, Accessed November 5, 2024.

3
Willing Vessel: God's Love for Humanity

From a young age, I sensed God's calling upon my life and felt a longing inside me to reach out to the lost, weary, and hopeless. My parents were committed to a church from my earliest years and entered full-time ministry while studying in Bible college, eventually becoming pastors after a few years. They remained in that church until my mid-twenties and later branched out to start their own ministry, dedicated to the Tamil-speaking community in Singapore. They were sincere in serving others and dedicated to helping many.

I left high school to work full-time in church. My school's vice principal was a kind, godly, inspirational woman. She wrote a good testimonial for me and gave her blessing as I embarked on this mission, even giving me opportunities to share my testimony with teachers and students in the school's morning assembly before I left.

Our church sent church planting teams with help, donations, and financial aid to various parts of the world. When a need arose in the East African country of Uganda, not many people were willing to go. Aware of the sacrifices, challenges, and possible dangers, my parents and I joined a six-person team, committed to accomplish the task set before us. At sixteen, I wanted to help the local people, especially the children and women.

During our time there, the rebels and the Karamojong (tribal warriors) caused significant trouble. People from nearby villages fled to our town for refuge from gun violence, rape, cattle theft, child recruitment and kidnapping, and slain men. Ebola hit in October 2000, and the people panicked. Thankful to be safe, alive, and well by God's Divine favor, protection, and grace, we remained, determined to fulfill our purpose there and to keep sharing God's love.

The experience felt like an adventure. I finally belonged and could do something my heart desired that was meaningful and greater than myself, even at my young age. As long as you are willing and available, God can flow through you. He will enable, equip, edify, and qualify you. Granting strength, wisdom, guidance, anointing, and discernment, He puts His love in your heart and works through you. Most importantly, He never leaves you in the mountaintop moments or the low valley experiences; He is faithful to carry you through, even if you make a mistake or take a wrong turn. As you continue to love and trust Him, He will turn things out for your good, rerouting you to the path you are meant to be on. In that process, so many valuable lessons are learned, growth begins, transformation occurs, and healing takes place.

Serving in Uganda made me cherish life more. Traveling the world and seeing how others live will make you thankful for the life you have: clean water, clothes, medication, sanitary napkins, bathrooms, clothes, food, and shelter. It was good exposure for me, instilling value, depth, and simplicity. Little did I know then that I would be globe-trotting as a flight attendant nine years later!

Africa was eye-opening. It was not easy but definitely worthwhile. I wanted to show people the love of Jesus; we prayed for and took care of the people, reaching out to the local community and welcoming them to church. I introduced the children to songs, played instruments, and taught them God's Word and was blessed with the opportunity to sponsor the education of a few teenage girls. I counted it a privilege to visit the sick, needy, and outcast. People do not care about how much you know; they want to see how much you care. I was committed to making a difference around me, even though it was far away from home with so many things to adapt to—climate, temperature, time zone, people, food. I contracted malaria four times.

The people in Uganda were hospitable and friendly. The children were so adorable and full of curiosity. Everyone there was musically inclined and creative. However, certain dangers were ever-present; and it was important not to draw attention to myself. I used no makeup, always had my long hair tied, wore long dresses or skirts, and secured my personal belongings. Women who wore pants were frowned upon. Break-ins and corruption were common. At times, we read in the papers or heard from friends about other people being stopped, robbed, shot, and raped at police or army checkpoints and roadblocks by criminals who were disguised as law enforcement officers or soldiers.

Nonetheless, Uganda is a country with an interesting way of living, colorful outfits, catchy music, unique mindset, and delicious food. The weather was hot and dry, and my skin darkened a few shades during our time there. I miss the beautiful, clear nights that made you feel like you could stretch out your arms and touch the stars because they seemed so close. The lack of skyscrapers made the view even more spectacular. On the other hand, I still get goosebumps, remembering all the insects that also live there. They were peculiar and bigger and nothing like I had ever seen in Singapore! Being there was an amazing experience with so much to get accustomed to. It was challenging yet rewarding in many ways.

It was a wonderful experience being in Uganda. It was challenging in many ways, yet rewarding and fulfilling. God was at work. Lives were being transformed; and people were being set free from alcoholism, polygamy, immorality, black magic, and witchcraft. The people were hungry for change, healing, and revival. It was beautiful to see families and relationships mended. Nothing is impossible for our God.

4
Unexpected: Alone and Afraid

My parents did not openly express their emotions; and in an atmosphere charged with tension, rules, restrictions, and physical discipline, I did not dare share mine for fear of getting in trouble. Despite that dynamic, they always provided food on the table, clothes on my back, and a clean home to live in.

I had a good education, and my parents instilled good values, respect, manners, and morals. Sadly, they did not model positive communication skills or understanding. I noticed the lack of affection toward me at the age of ten. My baby brother received plenty of hugs, kisses, and cuddles; I did not mind, as he was dear to me, too. After a certain age, looking into my dad's eyes became awkward, anyway, let alone the idea of hugging him. His extreme discipline, control, and lack of trust created a gap between us.

As kind and hardworking as my mom was, she did not convey love or warmth through touch. Hugs, kisses, and tender words made her uncomfortable; and perhaps her own upbringing factored into this element of her personality. Although I grew to be independent and self-reliant, she sometimes labeled me as attention-seeking if I needed her for something, while at the same time eagerly responding to my brothers for the same thing. It was weird and difficult, but I do not think she did it intentionally.

Even today, favoritism and partiality occur in Asian households, subtly or not. My mom and I approach many things differently; but she is a good wife, mother, and grandmother in her own way: prayerful, diligent, artistic, honest, and patient. She is also a good teacher by profession. For some people, maternal nurturing and open communication do not come naturally. I recognize my own strengths and weaknesses and have learned to embrace hers, loving her for who she is. We try to do the best we can with what we know and what we have. Thankfully, we have Jesus, and that makes a huge difference.

In her article "Not Every Mother Feels Like a Natural Mom—And That's OK," Sarah Bregel says that some women "are not born with the same deep maternal instincts . . . Some moms have to work a bit harder to embrace motherhood and all of its constant demands." She continues, "All our journeys as parents don't look exactly the same . . . It doesn't mean you aren't a real mother if being a mom doesn't complete you like you imagine it does for others . . . The range of emotions involved in parenting can be vast and overwhelming."[3]

Public speaker and counselor Gary Chapman wrote in his book *The Five Love Languages* that humans understand, receive, and express love through gifts, quality time, acts of service, physical touch, or words of affirmation.[4] My own love languages were not affirmed during childhood, especially after the age of ten. Combined with harsh physical discipline, this deficiency blurred my ability to

---

[3] Sarah Bregel, "Not Every Mother Feels Like a Natural Mom—And That's OK," Calm.com, https://carlm4kids.org/not-every-mother-feels-like-a-natural-mom-and-thats-ok/, Accessed June 27, 2024.

[4] Gary D. Chapman, *The Five Love Languages: How to Express Heartfelt Commitment to Your Mate* (Nashville, TN: Lifeway Press, 2010).

recognize the hallmarks of a healthy relationship. I could not discern the differences between love, control, or abuse—a drawback that continued to have an effect when I entered relationships in adulthood that were not good for me.

"The Lord is close to the brokenhearted; he rescues those whose spirits are crushed" (Psalm 34:18). At seventeen, I had never been allowed to entertain the thought of boys or talk about crushes, attraction, love, relationships, or sex; I could not have imagined that heartache and anguish were coming my way.

During our mission trip to Uganda, I genuinely cared about people and spreading God's love. I was also a teenaged girl, experiencing the normal developmental milestones of hormones, curiosity, infatuation, and a need for acceptance but had no one to talk with for advice and guidance. My parents were definitely unapproachable, and such a personal conversation with another team member would have been inappropriate.

I had just one close friend back home in Singapore, in addition to a few cousins that I was close to. Uganda's communication technology at the time offered only email (via dial-up internet access) and a landline that incurred extra fees for overseas calls. Privacy was also in short supply, since the devices were located in the house's common area—not to mention my hesitance to share anything that could get out among our friends and neighbors.

One of the local young men in the church participated in group music practices and Bible studies. Around four or five years older than I, he was friendly and helpful; and we began to talk. Soon, the occasional glance or exchange of smiles began to occur. These interactions led to holding hands briefly in secret and an occasional kiss. I wish that experience had not been my first experience.

He often stopped by my window at night to talk. Experiencing a man's interest for the first time after feeling unloved and unaccepted for so long made my awkward teenage self feel special. My dad's beatings and control tarnished my perception of a fatherly male figure, and I subconsciously yearned for love and acceptance from a man; as a result, I interpreted any form of male pursuit as affection and sincerity. He started to bring cards and overly perfumed plastic flowers on those evening visits, which made me feel noticed and wanted. Lonely and longing for connection, companionship, and admiration, I got a thrill of excitement from this attention.

One night, he asked if he could come into my room secretly. Unsure, I should have refused but did not know how. He lived in a guest house in our compound and often hung out at the big garage connected to the house. I did not know how to navigate the situation, realizing our paths would cross on a daily basis. Voicing concerns or questions about how to handle difficulties or resolve problems was not something I could do.

My feelings about his request were a combination of fear and guilt, and I knew something was not right. This dynamic was all new and confusing to me, but it could also feel wrong and weird. More than my body experiencing new things, my heart and mind were troubled. The adrenaline rush was nice at times, but the experience was not entirely pleasant.

Eventually, I let him into the house one night, not knowing what to expect but assuming we would talk and hold hands, maybe kiss or hug. I had never socialized with a male friend or been in a relationship and was really still a child: innocent, modest, naïve, and decent. To be honest, I do not know how I gathered enough courage to allow him into my room.

I was quiet, shy, and nervous; he was bold. We kissed, and he began to touch me in different places, making me uneasy. Things escalated; but despite my curiosity, it felt wrong. I believed in saving my virginity for marriage, both in obedience to God's Word and as a beautiful gift to unwrap with my husband one day. I was afraid—not ready for this. I wanted to undo everything, but there was no rewind button.

When he slowly moved toward me on the bed and made me recline, I said no, told him to stop, and made it clear that I did not want anything more to happen. But he did not care, ignoring all my protests. I continued to tell him to stop as he held me down, my tears flowing. Trying to push him away, I dared not scream for fear of getting in trouble. Undeterred, he persisted. I felt a sharp, piercing pain. At that moment, my heart broke; and it was as if something in me had departed.

I lay on the bed like a stone, feeling horribly foolish, disgusted, and angry with myself. When he was done with me, he left. I gently closed the door and crouched in the corner of my room, trembling and sobbing uncontrollably. I felt dirty and desolate, convinced God was displeased and would punish me for being a hypocrite and a failure.

Condemnation and guilt crept in, but the truth is that he had raped me. I had given no consent; furthermore, he did not use any method of protection. Still, I blamed myself: I had let him get close to me in the first place and then allowed him into my room. I hated myself for it. I felt scared and cut off from God. I just wanted it all to stop.

My parents were asleep in their room nearby, but I was too ashamed and afraid to call for help. They would not understand what happened and would blame me for "allowing" this to happen. My father might even hit me, saying it was my fault. He might hurt or even kill that person out of anger if he found out. All kinds of thoughts raced through my mind. I did not doubt my father's love for his daughter, but his pride and fear of what others thought would convince him that I had dishonored the family. I wished I could turn to him for comfort, protection, love, and assurance; instead, I suffered in silence to spare my family trouble.

Sadly, acquaintance rape—a sexual assault in which the survivor and perpetrator know each other, sometimes even intimately—is the most common form of rape. Embarrassment and the fear of being judged or not being believed prevent many women from revealing it has happened to them. But conviction and condemnation are not the same thing. The Holy Spirit convicts; the devil condemns. Conviction is beneficial and leads to repentance, change, forgiveness, healing, and peace. Condemnation breeds hopelessness, shame, hate, bondage, and misery. Conviction stems from God's love; condemnation stems from evil. Condemnation crept into my heart that day. I was filled with heaviness and sadness. I forgot that my Heavenly Father is not like my earthly father.

A few days later, he asked me to let him in again. For some strange reason, I agreed and lay like a corpse with no emotion or reaction as he repeated the offense. I felt dead inside, believing that since he already had me once, he could do it again. It was as if I did not care anymore. I felt broken and filthy inside.

Part of me also wondered if he really did like me; but even then, I had no idea what to expect or how to proceed. I was a total mess and did not know how to make it all stop. I was afraid of being punished and despised without anyone to turn to for help. I did know that I felt like I was losing myself; so when he returned, I gathered enough strength to refuse.

He was not pleased and tried opening my window from the outside by force. Terrified but resolved, I kept the lights switched off and remained quiet, hoping my parents would not hear the commotion. Thankfully, he did not manage to enter my room and left. Crying in bed from frustration, exhaustion, and fear, I prayed he would never speak to me or approach me again.

After a few weeks of feeling miserable and dreading the sight of him around the compound or at a church activity, I began to pull away from everyone; and it seemed that even God was no longer with me.

Talking about this time in my life still makes me cringe, even though my past does not define me. I wish I could go back in time to Uganda, hold young Grace in my arms, and assure her that she is not alone and that everything would be okay. What I can do is offer hope, healing, comfort, and encouragement through my story. Most importantly, I want my story to turn the hearts of people to God. He knows; He cares; He understands; and He will carry you through the storms of life. Your story is not over yet. God can transform your life.

God never turns away from us. He is not just the Creator of the universe but our truest Friend and Heavenly Father. He grieves and rejoices with us, knowing our fears, secrets, desires, and needs. He is our Comfort and Tower of Refuge, our Hiding Place, Pillar of Strength, and Anchor. He is our Help in times of trouble and Light in the darkness. He will never fail us; and even when we cannot see or feel Him, He is at work.

Sometimes, we may not understand everything that happens in our lives. Some circumstances strengthen our faith or prune our character, granting wisdom and strength for what lies ahead. Some consequences occur as the result of choices made. Regardless of the state we find ourselves in, nothing can happen in our lives without God allowing it. He is sovereign. He can turn our test into a testimony, our mess into a message. Trust His plan and purpose. Talk to Him and rest in His love. Step into the next season of life with boldness.

I know that as I continue to love and trust in the Lord, He will work things out for my good. He will restore all that is lost and give me beauty for ashes, fulfilling His purposes through me. "You intended to harm me, but God intended it for good to accomplish what is now being done, the saving of many lives" (Gen. 50:20). Take heart. God is in control. Your story is not over yet. Look ahead with hope, courage, faith, gratitude, and expectation.

I would like to add that *no* means *no*. Going on a date or inviting someone into your home is not consent. Any forced sexual activity is assault or rape. Communication, respect, and boundaries are important. No one asks to be violated, abused, or raped. Not everyone retaliates, runs, screams, or fights back. People do whatever is necessary to survive in that moment.

Parents, please keep an open line of communication with your children. Are you 100 percent certain that they are comfortable and brave enough to approach you, regardless of the situation? Make sure they know, understand, and feel your love—no matter how old they are or what they do. Remind your children that they can trust you and turn to you in every circumstance. You are their safe place. You are their glimpse of God's love and mercy.

Tell them that you will love, protect, and help them, even if you are upset or disappointed. Despite the consequences of their choices, you will still love them and be there for them every step of the way. Discipline, correct, guide, and teach from a place of love, understanding, and patience. Show them grace, forgiveness, and compassion. Reassure them of your love; you never know what tomorrow holds, and you cannot expect them to read your mind.

5
Dilemma: Please Don't Take My Baby

We returned home to attend church camp in Malaysia. Despite being surrounded by family and friends in a beautiful hotel, presented with a delicious buffet, I could not bring myself to eat anything but watermelon. As I looked at my exhausted reflection in the mirror, wondering why my jeans felt slightly tight around the waist, reality hit. I must be pregnant. Panicked, I kept the news to myself for the remainder of camp, after which we traveled to Singapore before returning to Uganda.

I shared everything that happened with my dear childhood friend, who was shocked and worried for me. Carla, as I will call her in this book, was a beautiful soul. Growing up, we spent time together whenever my father allowed it—during youth meetings at church, on music teams, through weeks of camp, and sometimes just to hang out. Although our lives differed greatly, she was always there to listen and laugh.

We bought a pregnancy test kit at the pharmacy, and my world came tumbling down when it came back positive. I confided in a close cousin, who later disclosed everything to an older cousin. Worried about the potential fallout with my dad and the effects on my future, they both advised me privately to have an abortion before anyone else found out. I was so confused, afraid, and mentally exhausted that their plan seemed like the only way out of the situation.

As the days went by, I spent a lot of time alone, thinking about what I wanted to do. For some weird reason, I strongly felt that the baby was a girl; and a little bond began forming between us. One night, crying uncontrollably in the bathroom, I realized I did not want to end a life forming inside of me. I knew that I was going to be in trouble with my parents, especially my father—that people would look at me differently and maybe disparage my family. They would judge, thinking I was promiscuous or rebellious.

I did not care anymore. "I will not let anyone take you away from me," I told her, placing my hand protectively over my belly. Even if no one agreed with me and everyone left me to face the consequences alone, I would keep the baby. The thought of being a mother brought me so much joy, and I knew that I would love the baby wholeheartedly.

I decided to gather all my courage and tell my parents the truth. The opportunity came one evening at church. The senior pastor's wife had noticed something was not right and privately asked me if everything was okay. Unable to hold it in anymore, I sobbed and told her I was pregnant. She cried and hugged me and offered to talk to my parents.

My head hung low in shame as I walked into the room where the three of them sat together. Tears stained my mom's face, but she hugged me. My dad looked sad, angry, and disappointed. His fists clenched in an effort not to reach out and slap me, and his first question was, "Why? Why, Grace? When did this happen?"

That question stung most. He did not ask me if I was hurt or what took place, so I knew that he already blamed me. His only concerns were why, when, and where. I wish I could have divulged everything to them at that point, but it felt like the situation was all my fault and that I had brought disgrace.

He decided the pregnancy would be terminated. My mom may have tried to appeal to him in private, but his face value and what people thought about the family were very important to him. Keeping the baby would bring dishonor and hinder his ministry. He made the appointment over my protests and forced me to go.

The consultation revealed that the pregnancy was eight weeks along. I told the doctor I did not want to proceed. He advised my parents to consider my input but noted that he understood I was young, and my parents' cooperation was crucial. My father booked the appointment for the procedure at a private hospital.

On the street outside the office, I wept and told my father I wanted to carry the baby to term and keep it. He broke down in public. It was the first time I had ever seen him cry. Falling to his knees, he begged me to terminate, saying he had never pleaded with anyone for anything; but he really needed me to have this abortion because he could not handle the pain and disgrace.

But that was not all. If I refused an abortion, he would leave my elder brother and me with my mother and go somewhere far away with my younger brother, who was only seven or eight years old. My little brother was dear to me. I had helped care for him since the day he was born, showering him with love and affection. I made up bedtime stories for him, and he would bang paintbrushes on biscuit tins to accompany me when I sang to him. I could not bear the thought of losing him.

I did not want to be the reason my family split any more than I wanted my mother to be caught in the middle. Why would I want to cause them more pain? Once again, I could not choose for myself, and my heart broke into many pieces when I finally agreed, promising myself that day I would not shed a tear. I hardened my heart in an effort to get through what was to come.

The nurse who tended me on the day of the procedure was neither kind nor friendly. She did remark that I should learn to keep my legs closed and not sleep around; I remained silent and dry-eyed. My parents seemed sad when they came to collect me. My body felt sore and uncomfortable, but the pain in my heart was even greater. For the next few hours, I struggled to come out of general anesthesia. Doctors and nurses were puzzled by my pleas that they not take my baby—the result of suppressed grief and anger. This after-effect has since resolved; but it was one more reminder of pain, loneliness, and loss.

Since our house was being rented during our mission term in Uganda, we spent the night with a family from our church. Sadly, my parents had to return to the field the next day. That night as they slept, I sobbed silently in the corner of the room. I needed my mother during this time. I did not know how to process everything that had happened, and the abortion affected me greatly. I needed her help. But their duties in Africa called, and they had to finish what they had started. They left Singapore with my younger brother the next day, and I was left with a big hole in my heart.

Somehow, I stayed strong and kept going one day at a time, knowing that I had to hold on to hope. As troubled as my mind was, I did not want to give up so easily. "In panic I cried out, 'I am cut off from the Lord!' But you hear my cry for mercy and answered my call for help" (Psalm 31:22). God would make a way for me. The couple that I was staying with was kind and caring while I struggled with pain, cramping, and excessive bleeding. After a few weeks of rest, I returned to working full-time at church, attending every service, Bible study, prayer meeting, team meeting, wedding, and funeral.

Although broken on the inside, I could still sense God's love and presence in my heart. In the midst of all the turmoil, confusion, and grief, I knew that I would somehow get through it. Busy with work, I kept in touch with my parents and looked forward to seeing my little brother again. I did not know what the future would hold, but I clung to God and trusted that something good could come out of it. Some days, I just wanted to disappear and give up; but through it all, He was my closest companion. The Holy Spirit kept urging me to hang on, reassuring me of God's unfailing love.

Processing the pain, loss, anger, and grief took time. Eventually, I chose to forgive my parents, especially my father. I also believe that the Holy Spirit would have convicted them as they continued their Christian faith. God sees and hears everything. He knows all things. He is just, merciful, and faithful. He is our Vindicator. He makes all things beautiful in His time.

I wish my parents would have showered me with love and assurance. As of this publication, they have yet to ask me what happened in Africa. In their minds, I let a man into my room and had sex with him; and the idea that anything else could have been the case has not seemed to occur to them. Many years later, I broached the subject with my mother, wondering why everything was swept under the rug like nothing happened, rather than dealt with and processed.

Acknowledging that they prayed for us kids regularly, I asked why they never checked on how I was doing or sought out counseling or therapy for me. She said nothing.

No perfect handbook on parenting exists. Each family, child, parent, and situation is different. It was not an easy situation for my parents. My father would have been concerned about how life would be for me, had I kept the baby. Sadly, the only thing he said was that he could not face the people in his family and the church. He had no strength to handle it. What was happening in my heart and inside our own family were not as important. The image portrayed to the public and how people viewed our family held priority.

I no longer blame my parents for their reaction. The root cause of their anger was hurt and fear. In painful or unexpected situations, even Christians can fail to act in accordance with God's Word. Some decisions require courage and grace. Maybe they thought they knew the best path for me; unfortunately, their choices caused more pain, chaos, turmoil, and heartache.

I am not saying that I would go back and change things in the past. I am thankful for the life I have now—grateful for where I am and who I have become on the inside. Everything that I have been through from the beginning has brought me to my daughter, Rania, and my husband, Joel. Honestly, now as an adult, I do not know how I would have managed, always remembering that I got pregnant as a result of rape. It probably would not have been a smooth journey, presenting challenges and frustrations.

But I also know that God, the Master Navigator, would have worked out the course of my life beautifully for me. With His help and grace, I would have gotten through it. I am His child and in the palm of His mighty hands. His plans for me are good, and He will fulfill His purposes in my life because I love and trust Him.

I have not forgotten my baby and believe that I will see her in heaven one day. Rest in peace, Laura Hope.

6
Preyed Upon: Make Your Stand, Grace

After what happened in Uganda, having the abortion, and remaining in Singapore, I was going through so much emotionally. Though I kept busy with work and church, I struggled on the inside; and being away from my parents at such a time was difficult. Staying at other people's houses was not comfortable, as it was never like my own home.

It was around 2001, and I was going along with the routine and requirements; but deep inside, it felt like I was sinking and a big mess. My emotions tangled together like a huge knot. I held tightly to God's love and promises but lacked proper support, stability, structure, love, and attention from my family.

I attended a Bible college called Asia Theological Center for Evangelism and Missions (ATCEM). It was good to learn in-depth about God's Word, grow in knowledge, and be involved in ministry. Through ATCEM, I met Pastor Chad Burton and his beautiful wife, Jennifer Brann Burton, a young couple from Texas who were based in Singapore at that time. He was funny, caring, authentic, and insightful; she was compassionate, friendly, genuine, and sweet.

Pastor Chad was one of my favorite lecturers, and I developed a nice friendship with them both that continues today. They became family to me, and their love and friendship carried me through that difficult year. They always listened and helped without judgment, making me feel seen, heard, understood, and accepted. They showed me God's love and grace.

Pastor Chad once said, "Live for an audience of one." That sentence has never left my heart and serves as a reminder for me to keep my eyes on God and to turn to Him first before anyone or anything else.

I faced various challenges on my own and wanted to be with my parents, who were hesitant to have me with them in Uganda after the previous events. Whether my persistence wore them down or they were worried about how much inner turmoil I experienced, I do not know; but eventually, they flew me back to Uganda. Before returning to Soroti, my parents dropped me off at the home of a nice family we knew in the capital city of Kampala in order to protect me from bumping into the guy who got me pregnant. The family was very gracious in opening their doors to us and many other missionaries over the years. I remained with the husband, wife, and two kids; and we had many pleasant moments.

They somehow felt like family, and I called them Uncle and Auntie. Auntie Mia (as I will refer to her) was always kind to me, and I enjoyed interacting with her. Her kids were younger than I was, and we often played together. That happiness was short-lived: the "uncle" whom I so respected—the Malaysian-born missionary, pastor, Ugandan tycoon, and CEO—chose to take advantage of me.

It started one night when everyone else was asleep in their rooms. I exited the bathroom and looked up to see him grinning at me from his recliner. He asked me to remove the socks from his feet. Requesting such a thing seemed really odd, but I wanted to give him the benefit of doubt. Confused and uncomfortable, I complied. He then grasped my hand and brought it to his mouth. I froze in embarrassment and shock, not daring to stand up for myself and clueless on how to react.

I felt heartbroken, violated, and betrayed. He was a father figure to me. I called him Uncle, and he abused that position to prey upon me. He was a husband, father, pastor, businessman, and prominent member of the community in his forties; I was eighteen. Still, I did not want to shout for Auntie Mia. I should have; but at that time, it was really hard. I was a guest in their home, at their mercy. I felt like a lost wanderer in a foreign land. I did not want to destroy their family. Their children deserved to be happy, safe, and at peace.

His exploratory groping became more aggressive. My heart started beating faster, and I quickly walked away to the kitchen under the pretense of getting a drink of water. Before I knew it, he grabbed me from behind, standing too close to mistake his intent. Nauseated with fear and unsure what to do, I squeezed free of his firm grip and hurried to the living room; but he came after me again, pulling me forcefully onto his lap as he threw himself on the couch. I froze. I felt like a complete idiot and wanted to cry. I wished someone would come to my rescue.

Twice I have heard God's audible voice and hope to hear it again someday. One morning around the age of eleven or twelve, I ran late while getting ready for school and missed my bus. The next one would arrive in just ten or fifteen minutes, but I would be late for class. Beginning to panic, I started praying in my heart that God would bring the bus sooner; so I could make it on time.

All of a sudden, someone spoke right next to my ear: "Haven't I told you in My Word not to waste your time, money, and talents?"

I was startled and almost took a step back, looking around to see who stood so close to me—but there was no one. I then knew it was God. That experience gave me goosebumps and left me feeling astonished and in awe. Thinking of many verses in the Bible that admonish us to make wise use of our resources—such as Matthew 25:4-30, Mark 12:41-44, Luke 6:38 and 12:48—I told God that I was sorry for not using my time well that morning. And just like that, the bus that was meant to arrive later appeared and stopped right in front of me!

I was sixteen the next time the audible voice of God came to me. I felt discouraged and weary one day, sitting on the floor by my bed in Uganda, with my head resting on one arm against the mattress.

"God, I cannot do much for you," I whispered.

Without hesitation, God spoke right back. "But I will do much through you."

Hearing His voice encouraged and uplifted me and brought me to tears. I knew that God would never walk away from me. He is always there, keeping His promises, through good times and bad.

I talk to God all the time, no matter where I am. The afternoon before Uncle Seth (as I will refer to him) violated me, I was spending time in prayer, as usual, when I felt God speak to me. It was not an audible voice but rather a strong prompting inside my heart—gentle, powerful, and clear. It said, "Uncle Seth is going to touch you tonight, Grace. You must make your stand."

I thought it was my imagination or maybe the devil and brushed the ridiculous thought aside, wondering why such an idea would enter my mind. As my prayer continued, the prompting returned; and I did not understand why God would give me such a warning if He could simply prevent the thing from happening. It made no sense, and I was afraid even to entertain the thought.

The truth is that God gives people free will. Though He convicts people and guides them toward what is right, they can still give in to temptation and make wrong choices. We may not understand everything that happens to us, but we can trust that God is good and faithful. He sometimes allows things for a greater cause: His purpose.

We may not always have all the answers and closure we feel is needed; but we can be at peace, knowing that He is sovereign and omniscient. It may be hard for you to see it right now, but everything will fall into place at the right time. All my life experiences have enabled me to write this book and touch the lives of others. Everything that I have been through can bring hope to people and direct them to Jesus. I want my story to magnify God's faithfulness and power.

That evening in Kampala, however, I felt confused, broken, and dirty. His breath was hot on my neck, and his hands traced a determined path on my skin. Clamping my jaw shut, I struggled to resist his demanding advances, which were physically painful, as well as emotionally horrifying and disgusting. Refusing to let me go, he redoubled his efforts; and his coercion intensified.

Suddenly, the words *make your stand* came to me, and I understood what they meant. If I remained in a frozen state of shock, he would eventually rape me. Galvanized, I broke free from his grip, pushed him back, and stood up. He was taken aback. I looked him in the eye and angrily asked him what his problem was. How could he do such things to me? I reminded him that he had broken my parents' trust. (My parents had even confided in him regarding my pregnancy and abortion.) I said he should be ashamed of himself, even more so because he had a daughter. Would he be okay if someone did the same to his child? I pointed out that he had betrayed his loving wife.

He looked at me with surprise, clearly feigning remorse while planning his response. His face and body language revealed that his apology was not genuine and he remarked that he thought that I would not mind because I seemed like a "happy-go-lucky girl."

I was furious. Who says that to someone they just sexually assaulted? I have no idea what he was trying to imply, but the offhanded comment upset me even more. When he realized his reasoning was not well-received, he apologized again and said he did not know what had come over him. He tried everything he could think of to prevent my telling his wife, attempting to manipulate me into believing that he genuinely believed he needed help. He acted like it all had happened so suddenly; he had no idea what had taken control of him.

Sadly, I knew that he was not truly remorseful; he was embarrassed, disappointed at my resistance, and afraid I would tell on him. He went on to elaborate how sorry he was and asked me to pray that he could change. He even pretended to cry with his hands over his face. When he could not manage to produce real tears, I recognized it for the act that it was. Getting him help, excusing him, and understanding his weakness were not my responsibilities. Uncle Seth was the abuser here; I was the victim.

I had a big heart; and people took advantage of it a lot, especially at such a vulnerable age. I was naïve; and because I was authentic with others, I also trusted people easily. He seemed to have discerned this and showed visible relief when I agreed to let it go and keep matters between us for the sake of his wife and children. I felt like the biggest idiot on the entire planet.

The next day, he left on a business trip as if nothing had happened, carrying on with his life without the burden of guilt or responsibility for his mistakes. He remained free from making things right, facing consequences, and experiencing justice or punishment.

I tried to pretend everything was okay, but the attack ate me up inside. I was an emotional wreck, crying or laughing to myself when I was alone. It felt like I was going crazy, and I wished I could run away and never return—just disappear. As I spent time with Auntie Mia and the kids, I felt like I was dying inside. Though I had done nothing wrong, I felt guilty, like it would be my fault if that family split up. A huge burden weighed upon my chest, and I did not know what to do.

As time progressed, my caffeine intake went from one cup of coffee per day to more than five and up to nine. I cried every time I was alone. The anxiety started to affect my stomach, and my digestion was disrupted anytime I ate. I was all at once lonely, uncomfortable, angry, and confused—desperate for help and intervention.

It was really difficult, but I knew that I had to take the first step if I wanted to heal. I had to do my part if I wanted any kind of change, and honesty is the best step forward. I could not allow uncertainty to cripple me any more than I could let Uncle Seth or his behavior take control of my life. I had to speak the truth and get help.

One morning, Auntie Mia and I sat chatting and laughing in the living room together; and it felt so nice to loosen up a little in the presence of her warmth and care that I wanted to do something special to bless her. She was experiencing some pain, so I offered to massage her feet in an effort to show her appreciation and love before our friendship came to an end.

I spoke to her about a "friend of mine" (the only way I could bring myself to tell her about everything that had happened to me). Auntie Mia was appalled. When she expressed her sadness for my friend, I asked if I could give her a hug, which seemed to confuse her, but she said yes. Realizing it would probably be our last hug, I started to weep. She asked me what was wrong, but I could not stop crying and did not know how to tell her. I did not want to hurt her.

I finally gathered enough courage and said, "You know the story I just told you? Well, that girl is actually me."

Auntie Mia's face changed. The first thing she asked was, "Who is the man in the story?"

My heart sank. I learned that she suspected her husband's brother, who lived in the same country and had a playful disposition. She asked me again with so much pain in her voice. Tears filled her eyes when she heard her husband's name. I could see anger, shock, and sadness on her face.

"No, no, no!" she cried. "How could this be? How could he do this to you? We have had so many people stay in our house over the years, and some of these women would even walk to the kitchen wearing just a big shirt. And now I am wondering if you were the first one he has behaved inappropriately with. I wonder if he has done this before. He has helped and interacted with so many women and children. I can't believe this, Grace. How could my husband do such a thing to you? And why you? I don't know what to say. What am I going to tell your parents? You're just a child, and we have a daughter, too!"

Walking past Auntie Mia's room that night, my head hung low, I could hear her loud wails. It broke my heart to have brought her such bad news. Abuse does that sometimes: people do bad things to you, yet you feel like you are to blame. Many times, it is the abuser who makes you feel that way. Do not allow it. It is not your fault. My heart hurt for Auntie Mia and for myself. As a wife and mother, I can now empathize how she would have felt. What a painful situation to be in!

I could not sleep that night. My heart felt heavy, and I wanted to run away. But where could I go? I was in a foreign land, living in the house of my abuser. Now his wife knew, and she planned to confront him when he returned the next day. Where could I hide? I wished that I would go to sleep and never wake up.

I asked God what my purpose was and why I had even been in Uganda in the first place. So much mess had occurred in my life—first the pregnancy, then the abortion, and now this. My desire was to reach out to the local people, to help them, and to show them God's love. I knew that I was sincere and genuine in all that I did and that my time in Africa was not a mistake. I believed that everything passes through the hands of God first, and nothing happens without His knowing.

I still felt like a failure and a joke. Despair and uncertainty filled my heart. I told God that I was a mess and that being in Uganda was pointless. I was useless. Hitting rock bottom, I said, "God, why am I even here? What is the point of it all? I have achieved nothing. My life means nothing." I cried myself to sleep.

Suddenly, my eyes flew open; and I saw myself floating away from my body, while my spirit was lifted up and away. Two massive beings stood beside me, one on my left and one on my right. They were so huge and tall that I could not see past their waists. I believe they were angels. They did not say much. I was very confused and thought that maybe I had died. I asked the angels what was happening and where they were taking me. They told me to wait and see for myself.

We reached another place rather quickly. I saw a long stretch of road before me. Everything seemed foggy, and the path ahead was gold. The angels told me to keep walking; and I saw thousands of people, representing a multitude of different colors, genders, nationalities, and races.

As I walked further, the angels said, "Now look and observe." People I never met smiled and waved at me eagerly, their faces full of joy and gratitude. As I got closer, they shouted out to me, saying things to me like, "Grace! Grace! Thank you. I am here today because of you! Thank you, Grace. Because of you, we know Jesus. If not for you, we would not have known about God. We are here because of you. Thank you, Grace, for your life. I am here because of what you did."

I could not believe it. I was surprised and overwhelmed with everything I saw and heard. My body jolted awake; and I trembled on the bed, tears flooding down my face. I felt so feverish, and I was trembling. That encounter ministered to me deeply. God showed me that my life was not in vain and reassured me of His love, reminding me of how my life made a difference. I knew that He would fulfill His purposes for my life and flow through me as I continued to surrender myself and make my heart available to God. No one and no painful situation should discourage me from touching lives.

I am truly thankful for that experience. I know that God is with me, faithful to carry me through every situation in life. His plans for me are good. I need to stay the course. The only one that can keep me down is me. I need to rise up, have faith, and fight the good fight. Holding on to hope, I must gather courage and move forward, believing better days are ahead. God is not finished with me yet. My story isn't over.

> O Lord, you have examined my heart and know everything about me. You know when I sit down or stand up. You know my thoughts even when I'm far away. You see me when I travel and when I rest at home. You know everything I do. You know what I am going to say even before I say it, Lord. You go before me and follow me. You place your hand of blessing on my head. Such knowledge is too wonderful for me, too great for me to understand! I can never escape from your Spirit! I can never get away from your presence! If I go up to heaven, you are there; if I go down to the grave, you are there. If I ride the wings of the morning, if I dwell by the farthest oceans, even there your hand will guide

me, and your strength will support me. I could ask the darkness to hide me and the light around me to become night—but even in darkness I cannot hide from you. To you the night shines as bright as day. Darkness and light are the same to you.

You made all the delicate, inner parts of my body and knit me together in my mother's womb. Thank you for making me so wonderfully complex! Your workmanship is marvelous—how well I know it. You watched me as I was being formed in utter seclusion, as I was woven together in the dark of the womb. You saw me before I was born. Every day of my life was recorded in your book. Every moment was laid out before a single day had passed. How precious are your thoughts about me, O God. They cannot be numbered! I can't even count them; they outnumber the grains of sand! And when I wake up, you are still with me! (Psalm 139:1-18).

Worried and anxious, I stayed inside my room the night Uncle Seth returned from his business trip. Auntie Mia confronted him as soon as he entered the house. He denied it initially but confessed as she kept questioning him. I heard her slap him hard. She was crying and asking him why he had done such a thing.

"We have a daughter, too!" she exclaimed. "How could you do this?"

He claimed not to know what had happened. He said something had come over him while he was watching television; and a black, shadowy figure had taken control of him, which is what he eventually told my parents, too.

Auntie Mia made him apologize to me in person. I felt so awkward, uncomfortable, and embarrassed. With time, I became numb and felt no emotion. I think it was my mind's way of dealing with things and protecting myself as I held tightly to my sanity.

The next day, Auntie Mia and Uncle Seth made the five-hour drive to Soroti to see my parents, where she made him confess everything; and they both pleaded for forgiveness. I can imagine how horrible Auntie Mia would have been feeling: the agony of one mother telling another what happened to her daughter. I know the news would have shattered the hearts of any parents.

That evening, they returned with my little brother and our parents, who spoke to me privately to find out what had happened. I remember feeling so embarrassed to tell them everything, especially in front of my father, and could not hold back the tears. I felt humiliated and distraught, but I knew as parents they wanted to know all the details.

I know they were hurt by this incident. It must have been a very painful and challenging period for them. They told Uncle Seth how disappointed they were with him and that he had broken their trust. They said they forgave him, although it was hard to do so. My parents then proceeded to tell me how strong and brave I was and that I should forgive him, too. They made me say it out loud. It was an unwise discussion, especially with Uncle Seth present; and everything was being settled too soon.

I could not understand what was happening. Why were such things taken so lightly and handled quickly? Was it for my well-being and the best thing to do at that time? Or was it for the ease of everyone else? Was it to ensure that none of this ever got out (just like my pregnancy)? Was it to protect my father's pride and face value? Was it to protect Auntie Mia and her children?

I understand and agree that, as Christians, we are to forgive. The Bible says in Romans 12:19 that vengeance belongs to the Lord. I wish Uncle Seth and his family no harm and want to show mercy. Holding on to bitterness and refusing forgiveness will destroy me. I need to release that pain and anger to God (and still do). Sometimes that process takes time, and sometimes it can be done instantly. Every situation differs.

What I did not like was how the incident was being handled. It did not bring me any relief, comfort, or assurance. I did not get the justice, help, or support I needed. Perhaps my parents did not know what to do at that point with so much happening over a short period of time. I think they were in a dilemma, themselves.

They chose to leave me in Uncle Seth's house for a while, this time with my little brother, as well. Although it was nice to have him around—and Auntie Mia remained—I felt uncomfortable, uneasy, and fearful to live with Uncle Seth in his house. I began looking at the door to my room at bedtime, worried that he might appear at night. Anxiety significantly disrupted my sleep. I wondered what he would have done to me on the night of the abuse if I had not stopped him, and having those thoughts in my head was disturbing.

Some days, it felt in a weird way like I was getting used to being around him. I was developing Stockholm syndrome and started contemplating if I had done anything to tempt him or encourage his behavior, gradually beginning to blame myself. I had to find ways to get rid of these mentally exhausting thoughts.

Uncle Seth started getting comfortable again; and I would catch him looking at me in a lustful way, smiling at me sometimes and getting me to pass him items like the television remote, salt shaker, butter dish, or newspaper. He was becoming too relaxed. Once, we were all watching television, and he playfully threw a cushion at me on the couch. I did not know how to react. Auntie Mia shouted at him. Poor woman, it must have been hard on her to deal with such a husband.

Finally, the day arrived when my parents took my little brother and me back to Soroti with them. They would have continued their ministry in Africa if none of this had ever happened, and I think they had no other options left. It was good to be home as a family. My parents continued working in church; and I remained a member, participating in the worship ministry and maintaining a low profile. People in Soroti wondered why I was suddenly different toward them, keeping to myself and spending most of my time with my little brother. I could not tell anyone anything. We eventually left for Singapore and never returned to Uganda.

I shared what happened in Uncle Seth's home with another pastor and his wife a few months after the incident. They were shocked and brought the matter up to my senior pastor's wife, whom I had loved and respected since my earliest years. She and her husband had come to Singapore from the United States as missionaries many years ago. They were good, sincere, hardworking people. They were generous, compassionate, and nurturing. Their hearts were for people and missions.

I vaguely remember a conversation with my senior pastor's wife, my parents, and perhaps another pastor. Sadly, she told my parents she found out about what had happened through someone else. She was probably referring to the pastor and his wife to whom I had opened up. I do not know if she thought I was attention-seeking, but she turned toward me angrily and asked, "Did you like it? Did you like what he did to you? Because you should have just slapped him hard on his face. I told my children the same thing when they were young; that if someone touches them inappropriately like that, just turn around and slap him hard. Why did you not do that?"

I was shocked and hurt by the things she said. It felt like a knife had gone through my heart that day. Her questions embarrassed me, and I realized that she could not possibly understand what I had undergone. If a boy my age or someone younger tried to grope me, I could have easily shouted at him and punched him in the face, but I was a teen at the mercy of a grown man in his forties. I was away from my family, a guest in the perpetrator's home. His actions stunned, frightened, humiliated, and disgusted me. Yes, I panicked and froze initially, but I did put an end to it eventually when I made my stand.

Already devastated, I was hurt further, knowing people did not believe or understand me. When people in authority, especially those in church leadership, talk to you like that, it makes you not want to open up to anyone ever again. This reaction is one of many that prevent victims of abuse from speaking up; they either suffer silently, deal with it on their own, move on quietly, or wait many years to gather courage and make their voices heard.

My pastor's wife had no bad intentions, and she probably did not mean to come across that way. People make mistakes. Asking me if I liked it, however, really was a slap on my face that made me feel degraded. She should not have spoken to me that way, particularly in her position. Her words could easily have been a stumbling block to me.

What hurt even more was my parents chose not to stand up for me at the time, even though it would have been hard for them to say anything, far less tell her off; not only was she much older, but she was also technically their boss. I still wish my parents had prioritized my well-being.

As we were heading home that afternoon, my dad said, "You see, Grace, sometimes you think you can open up to others; but not everyone will understand you or give you the response you want. It's okay. Only God will understand you."

I remained quiet, my head hung low. I did not know what to say, think, or feel anymore; and the journey was lonely. Thankfully, I kept hanging on to God. Forgiving my pastor's wife fully took some time, but I have learned not to harbor grudges. I want to get better, not bitter. Changing people is God's job, not mine.

People, especially adults, need to be held accountable for their choices, whether they accept correction, seek counseling, or make amends. No action was taken against Uncle Seth within the church, nor was a police report made. If I am correct, I believe he never did step down from his roles, and the whole thing seemed to have been swept under the rug. I worry whether he has done this to someone else before. Are there other women who have been too ashamed or afraid to speak up?

Has Uncle Seth truly repented? Only God knows! Were things kept quiet because personal and public dynamics would have become too complicated and messy? Were my parents trying to avoid further turmoil in my life? Or was it just the easiest and least disgraceful solution for everyone? Was Uncle Seth corrected privately? I do not know.

None of what they did helped me or ensured that I got therapy or counseling. It did not seem fair that I was forced to self-heal, which affected so many years of my life. But by the grace of God, here I am today, stronger and wiser. I am not defined by my trauma, and you are not defined by yours.

I chose to forgive Uncle Seth and to leave the matter in God's hands. If he has truly repented and changed his ways, well, good for him. But if he is still unremorseful and sleazy, then may God chastise him and have mercy on his family. We all have to answer God one day. Only He knows the true condition of our hearts. I wish Uncle Seth no harm, and I pray that God will help him.

People often leave the church or lose their faith in God when another Christian hurts them, saying that Christians are hypocritical, judgmental, and proud. In doing so, we fail to remember that Christians are flawed humans, too. Just as some Christians do not have a close relationship with God and give in easily to their sinful nature, others are good, God-loving Christ-followers who flow in the love of God. The most important thing to remember is to keep our eyes on Jesus, the Author and Perfecter of our faith (Heb. 12:2).

Our walk with God cannot depend on how other Christians treat us; rather, we need to establish our own relationship, spending time with Him and growing in His Word. He is our Firm Foundation. Everything that can be shaken will fall apart, but God will never fail us. When we look to other people, we can sometimes be disappointed or betrayed. Look unto the Lord and trust Him. Keep your eyes on Him. He will never let you down. He will never put you to shame.

I have no idea what happened to Auntie Mia, her family, or her marriage. Maybe they are still together. I recently saw videos and articles of interviews with Uncle Seth online, talking about business, pastoral ministry in Uganda, and other success tips—all lauding his achievements and praising what a wonderful person he is. My stomach turned with feelings of pain, injustice, anger, frustration, and disappointment when I saw these things. I cried out to God, releasing the burden in my heart to Him, my Healer.

My life is in His hands. His plans for me are good. I am not defined by my trauma. I am no longer a victim but more than a conqueror in Christ Jesus. I have hope, victory, healing, redemption, blessings, favor, peace, and joy.

I have boldness. I have a purpose.

If you have experienced violence, sexual assault, humiliation, or any kind of abuse, you do not have to be ashamed or live in condemnation. Your worth is not based on your reproductive organs, body, virginity, chastity, or marital status. You are precious and valuable. Be strong, courageous, and confident.

Families, especially parents, should not make their sons or daughters feel ashamed of the pain they experience at the hands of others. This reaction happens to a lot of people, mainly girls and women in households of certain ethnicities, whose cultures consider it a disgrace when their daughters are molested, raped, harassed, abused, divorced, separated, cheated on, or become single moms. Sometimes, they even blame her—they claim it is because of what she wore, how she behaved, where she went, how she looked, or what she said. It is a heartbreaking and worrisome period for the whole family, but why blame the victim? Do not justify abuse, infidelity, or assault.

Some parents consider it great shame, placing that burden on the victim (whether it be a child or adult). One of my aunts learned that I was physically abused in a relationship, and the first thing she asked me was, "What did you do in order for him to hit you?"

I was shocked and disappointed at her question because she was a wife, sister, mother, grandmother, and prayerful Christian. I did not expect her to respond this way. Upset, I asked her how she could say something like that. Violence is wrong. She said she was only trying to understand the situation better. I asked if she were the type of person who would tell a woman she was raped because of what she was wearing, and an awkward silence fell over the room as, ironically, my aunt got offended. I forgive her.

Focusing on your pride, ego, or status is irrelevant, immature, selfish, and unloving. The situation is not about your dignity as parents, who have no reason to hide in shame or wallow in misery. The people who need to be embarrassed and ashamed are the ones who commit the crimes. Families need to uplift, support, understand, forgive, help, and stand by the one who suffers, giving encouragement and love. Show grace and compassion. Pray with and for them. Stay strong with your hurting child or sibling, so he or she can heal and find stability once again. Do not sweep things under the rug or pretend the thing never happened. Expressing emotions is okay. Talk with your children, get them the help they need, support their journey to recovery, and show them what bravery means. Get help together, if needed.

The people who need to be ashamed are the men who abuse, sexually assault, circulate intimate videos, or tarnish the reputation of women. They should be afraid and embarrassed for what they have done, and their parents should be disappointed at the kind of men their sons have become. Shame and defeat should not be placed on the victims. What I write applies to both male and female perpetrators, who should live with the guilt of their actions until they have shown true remorse, sought forgiveness, repented, and gotten therapy.

If you are reading my book right now and are hurting or have had a painful past, I want you to know that you can get through this. You are so wonderfully complex. You are God's workmanship, beautiful and worthy. I know it seems hard now, but it will all get better in due time. I understand how it feels. Please do not lose hope. Rise up. Be bold. Hold your head high. You are no longer a victim. You may be a survivor, but you are victorious. With God's help, you can overcome this and emerge stronger. Do not give your abusers the power to keep you down and destroy your whole life.

Do not let the devil rob you of your joy, peace, faith, and strength. You are a conqueror, and nothing can separate you from the love of Jesus. You are not alone.

"No, despite all these things, overwhelming victory is ours through Christ, who loved us" (Rom. 8:37).

7
Divorce 1: Defiled and Broken

Domestic violence can damage you mentally, emotionally, and physically. Monsters do not hide under beds—they can exist in real life, and you meet them. Dax (as I will call him) seemed fun in the beginning; but deep inside, he was insecure, proud, hot-tempered, and lustful. He inflicted so much pain and filth in my life during our time together. Maybe he was full of misery and darkness. Maybe he never dealt with his inner demons. Or maybe he was just too egotistic and arrogant to work on himself. Only God knows.

We started hanging out when I was eighteen, shortly after my return to Singapore from Uganda. A decade older than me, he was Singaporean like myself; and our families attended the same church for many years. He was with the Special Operations Command (police task force). His ex-wife had taken their child and left him within a year of the marriage to go back to a previous boyfriend, whom she later married. According to her, Dax had never laid his hands on her.

Ideally, he would not have been someone that I would have considered dating or marrying; but I did not have a healthy understanding of a man's love or good relationships at the time, instead subconsciously associating abuse with love. He had the bad boy image, and there were so many red flags about him. He was good with art, making things with his hands, and cooking; and he loved to joke. But he was also chauvinistic, flirtatious, playful, and always seemed to tease women, especially teenage girls.

I soon discovered that he had major anger issues but, believing that everyone deserved a second chance, chose to overlook them and focus instead on his good qualities (which were few). I thought he could change for the better, given the right circumstances, and that love could accomplish that. While love is amazing, beautiful, and powerful, only God can truly transform. People need to make right decisions and choose wisely. Love will produce no positive result if a person refuses to acknowledge that he or she has an issue or needs help. Change has to come from within.

Though my parents initially did not approve of our dating and forbade our relationship, they eventually gave their support and blessings, knowing I was determined. Deep inside, they could have been afraid I might become sexually involved with Dax or get pregnant outside of marriage, so they brought up marriage talks with his family within a year. I wish they had given us more time to date or insisted that we take more time to get to know each other better. Delaying marriage plans may not have prevented a sexual relationship, but it might have discouraged me from marrying him and saved me from the torture that was to come.

Sadly, however, some parents of Asian or other ethnicities sometimes rush kids who are in relationships into marriages because they want to prevent gossip or protect their family name, self-respect, and pride. They also want to ensure their children do not get pregnant out of wedlock or engage in premarital sex. While these concerns are understandable, I think if parents and children have a good, healthy, loving bond, they can handle situations with good communication, trust, unity, understanding, and connection. Moving quickly into marriage is not the best solution. Parents should learn to put their faith in God, trust the process, and guide their children patiently through each step.

I spent almost six years with Dax—years filled with more tears than laughter. He was not someone I would have become involved with if I had been emotionally secure; but I was vulnerable, broken, and deeply hurting from the events of the last year. I felt unloved, lonely, used, unworthy, and unwanted and thought no one would ever accept me if they knew what happened to me. I also wanted to get away from a strict and controlling dad, who made me feel as though I could not breathe.

On the night of our wedding, Dax became angry over some minuscule thing and took the bed, leaving the floor for me. As time went on, he hit and sexually violated me often, grooming me for things I had never been exposed to before. Trying to protect and understand him, I thought keeping most of it a secret was being a good partner. I was wrong. He was vile, disrespectful, and selfish. He was inconsistent, immature, perverted, and abusive—in a good mood one day and filled with rage the next—and there was no way to know what would upset him. He was like a ticking time bomb.

Dax was selfish and controlled everything I did. He offered no sincere love, respect, care, or commitment. Sex occurred only when he wanted it. Most days, he watched pornography or movies that contained nudity and sexual scenes. Being a newly married twenty-year-old, I felt unloved, undesired, and unappreciated. Some nights, he hated having me around and waited for me to go to bed, so he could watch pornography in secret and take care of his own needs. His behavior seemed absurd to me, and I was hurt and confused.

During that time, I worked for three years in a semi-government organization that housed and helped abused children and juveniles, aged four to sixteen, and later spent a year with another organization that helped struggling families. I continued to serve faithfully at church—helping out, playing instruments, and singing each week—but inside, I was broken and suffering in silence. Telling anyone I was married to a wolf in sheep's clothing was hard; and I was confused, hurting, in denial, afraid, ashamed, and trying to make things work. If I refused or went against him, he would hit me, verbally abuse me, or withhold all forms of affection.

I was lonely, yearning for love, and afraid of being unwanted. Although God was with me all along, pain blurred my outlook. I was trapped in a cycle of abuse: leaving the marriage meant returning to a caring family who did not support me in some ways. My mother took care of me. My dad was a good provider but strict, overprotective, opinionated, and controlling. Even as an adult, I did not want to go back to living under the roof of a man who was such a harsh disciplinarian from the time I was around nine or ten until I was fifteen. So I remained in the abusive relationship with Dax, wanting independence and the opportunity to make something out of my life. But I was with the wrong person.

He punched, kicked, and slapped me, dragged me by my hair, humiliated me in public, and constantly shouted at me. I was degraded, verbally abused, and neglected. He frequently used profanity while threatening, insulting, and calling me names. He filled my life with uncertainty and sadness. Using basically anything he could get his hands on to hit me (in addition to using his hands and feet), he reached for belts, wooden poles, pillows, a wristwatch, or a motorcycle helmet. The result was painful bruises, wounds, scratches, concussions, blood clots, sore limbs, a broken finger, punctured scalp, dizzy spells, body aches, swollen eyes, and fever.

Sometimes after I cooked a meal, he threw the plates and cups at me. I then spent the entire night clearing the pieces of broken glass and the food that splattered walls and carpets, while he left the house or went to bed. I cried often and developed sleep paralysis, accompanied by disturbing nightmares. While in that state, it was hard to determine if what I saw was real or just an eerie dream.

I prayed about it daily, trusted God for an intervention, and reached out to godly friend and loved ones for prayer, patiently believing I would receive healing and deliverance. Twenty years later, the breakthrough happened. God came through for me.

Several times, he demanded in anger that I get off his motorbike and proceeded to leave me stranded on the highway without personal belongings, phone, wallet, or keys. I walked all the way home in shame and sadness. Once in a while, I called my dad; and even though we have not always seen eye-to-eye, he would come pick me up. My dad was always there when I needed help but did not want to make matters worse by unleashing his anger on Dax for everything he did to me. His involvement in church ministry meant he had to be mindful of his ways, so he practiced self-control with the desire to ensure that my marriage would thrive.

Dax's behavior made me feel unattractive, and I wondered if something was wrong with me. I began to equate my value with how he treated me. Despite being a beautiful, talented, eloquent young lady, I felt flawed, unimportant, and insecure when I was with him.

I never experienced true intimacy. Dax experimented his sexual fetishes on me and would sometimes hit me if I refused or questioned his actions. He emotionally manipulated me and withheld physical touch if I did not comply with what he wanted. Some days, it seemed as though we were okay together; and our day would go well. We spent time with family and friends. Soon, however, the nonsense began again. It was not a healthy, wholesome marriage; it was destructive.

He made me feel uncomfortable and dirty on the inside. As a young Christian woman, I dealt with much condemnation because of the things he introduced me to—pornography, alcohol, and clubbing. He was a smoker, and I developed the habit while we were dating. I started to enjoy it, and smoking became a part of my lifestyle. I carried cigarettes with me everywhere and hung out with friends who smoked.

Thankfully, I quit the habit completely after nine years by God's grace and help and my own determination, self-care, and willpower. I faced withdrawal symptoms (mental and physical) but did not give up. One day, I put a cigarette in my mouth and almost gagged when I went to light it. I could not stand the smell, taste, or sight of it. Feeling sick, I could not bring myself to take even one puff. Just like that, I lost all interest in smoking. That was truly our miracle-working God's doing.

Despite all of Dax's mistreatment, I held on to faith and did not let go of God. It was a rocky journey. I tried my best to trust Him while actively participating in church, praying, and reading the Bible often; but I was torn apart inside. I felt like a sheet of white paper that had been crumpled and trampled on, soon to be shredded and discarded. Being married to a man who made me feel like I had to obey everything he said in order to be a good wife and safeguard the marriage was a constant struggle. He betrayed my trust and dishonored our wedding vows, while I craved love and did whatever I could to please him.

Dax dictated how I should dress when he took me to clubs, selecting the skimpiest outfits and getting mad if I did not wear what he chose. He often insisted that we show public affection late at night in quiet, dark parks where sleazy men wandered around or hid in bushes. If I refused, he would stop showing me any kind of love or physical touch. He found ways to manipulate me, saying he engaged in such activities only with me, since I was his wife; he was not like other men who cheated on their wives. He made me believe I needed to fulfill his every desire if I wanted him to remain faithful. He had a sick mind and messed me up on the inside.

Once, Dax booked a massage appointment for me. When I arrived at the dodgy spa, I was required to completely undress with only a little towel to cover my private parts. The massage therapist was a man, and Dax had arranged to sit in the room and observe. He did not hide his enjoyment in watching the man massage my entire body, even climbing over me to massage my back. I felt horribly uncomfortable, especially when Dax stepped out for a few minutes. Thankfully, nothing untoward took place in the room; however, the masseur complimented how attractive I was and asked me to return for more appointments because he enjoyed the experience.

I was shocked and appalled when Dax started taking me to the red light district late at night, looking for dark areas to have sex. I had never gone to those places and did not want to be there. Hesitant, I asked why we had to be there when we lived in a beautiful apartment. But he was unrelenting.

The red light district was disturbing and pungent. It reeked of sewage, urine, and other bodily fluids. You could sense foul, unclean spirits in the area. It was eerie. When I walked through those dark alleys, the shutters of closed shops sometimes shook and vibrated, as if something else was present in those places but could not come near me. My hair stood on end. My heart felt heavy, even as I muttered the name of Jesus under my breath. I felt so lost.

I now understand that even during those painful, dirty, scary, and unpleasant moments, God was watching over me. "Even when I walk through the darkest valley, I will not be afraid, for you are close beside me. Your rod and your staff protect and comfort me" (Psalm 23:4).

Being in the red light district with Dax was mentally torturing. I could see silhouettes of people (prostitutes and customers of both genders) who were having sex. Men looked at me lustfully when I walked past. Dax ushered me to remote corners and asked me to perform sexual acts on him, labeling me boring or insubmissive if I refused to go along with what he wanted. When I did comply, men often watched from hiding places while pleasuring themselves. Sometimes, they approached us and tried to touch me from behind. Cringing, I told Dax to stop it, but his opinion was that they could watch or touch me just a bit. They could never have me, since I was his. He instructed me to keep still and ignore them. My pervasive fear of being beaten or abandoned trapped me into obedience.

One night, Dax drove me around the red light district and asked if I wanted to have sex with other women while he watched. He parked near a pimp and some working girls, appearing eager to organize something, so he could take pleasure in watching. Fortunately, nothing he desired worked out that day. I eventually told him that I did not want to proceed with it. Though disappointed, he did not get angry; and we left.

Constantly surrounded by abuse and sexual exploitation, I was beginning to lose myself and did not know what to do. He was slowly turning me into something that I was not. He unleashed all his baggage and filth on me over the years. No good husband who truly loves, values, and cherishes his wife would do such a thing. I felt unloved and taken advantage of and cannot recall any good or decent times we had together.

Dax messed with my mind, heart, and life. I foolishly believed that things could get better, that he would change. I did everything I could to fix the marriage and appease him, but it was all in vain. He was danger. He was damaging. He was deadly. And I had to get away from him.

Miraculously, we were not able to have a child together, despite trying to conceive. It was definitely a blessing in disguise. Of course, Dax blamed me. He said that I was barren, and my womb was cursed. (I think people like him should never reproduce.)

Our marriage finally ended when I found multiple missed calls after midnight on his phone from a girl under sixteen years old. Angry at being discovered and questioned about it, he beat me, threatened to kill me, and broke many things in the house before grabbing a belt with a big buckle and giving me five minutes to leave. He said he would kill me if I stayed longer. I escaped with a Nike bag on my shoulder that held only a tissue packet, comb, phone charger, mobile phone, wallet, keys, and a tiny bar of soap.

My heart was broken. I hurt physically, mentally, and emotionally and could not see or think clearly anymore. I walked and walked without knowing where I was going, thoughts of suicide filling my mind. I wanted to end my life, though I did not know how.

As I walked, I thought about many things. I knew that I should not take my own life as it was given by God, but I felt so much despair. My parents and especially my younger brother, then a teenager, came to mind; and I remembered all the good times he and I had. I did not want to scar him for life. If I did something stupid to myself, my family would hurt greatly.

Choosing to be strong and patient, I called a cousin, who followed me to the hospital. The doctor saw the bruises Dax caused and asked if I wanted to call the police. Saying yes was a tough, scary decision for me. I made a police report but said not to press charges, telling them I would file for a personal protection order (restraining order). I know now that I should have pressed charges against him, but making that decision in that moment was difficult.

At the police station the next day, the investigating officer did not seem to take me seriously. It felt like he kept trying to downplay the situation—perhaps he was a male chauvinist himself, or maybe he was trying to help Dax, who was also in the police force. Less bold than I am now, I went away silently with a restraining order.

The family court mandated counseling, and I showed up for every session, foolishly hoping Dax would show some remorse. He was cold, stone-hearted. In his mind, he was right; and he had the upper hand. He informed the counselor he did not love me anymore and wanted the marriage to be over.

Sadly, Dax knew I was weak and afraid and that I still cared about him. Despite the restraining order against him, he beat me up in public again after our separation, when we were no longer living together. Displeased at having spotted me out with friends one evening, he later found me and began to hit me, dragging me by my hair on the pavement. He snatched my belongings, including my phone and keys, and ripped my clothing. I managed to break free from his grip, run away, and escape in a cab.

Divorce proceedings soon began. He continued to bully me throughout the legal process and sale of the house. Although the property did not yield much profit, I decided to split the share equally, which angered him even further because he wanted to leave me with nothing. His family took his side and blamed me for making a police report and getting a restraining order. He had already begun sleeping with another woman.

Ending the relationship with Dax brought great relief. I was finally free of him and could feel safe without enduring any more torture. I was a complete mess, but at least he was out of my life. At some point, he was forced to resign from the police force after being charged with indecent exposure. Recently, I learned that he is being investigated for molesting three girls who are minors. I hope justice and truth will prevail.

I struggled with insecurity, low self-worth, loneliness, and anger after the divorce. It was hard to think straight; and I did not live wisely, seeking validation in the wrong places and making foolish choices along the way. But God, in His mercy, turned things around.

His grace, love, and sovereignty changed the course of my life. He rerouted my steps, and I could rebuild my life again. After everything came to an end in 2008, I could finally move on with my life, though I had no clear direction of what I should do next. I hung on to Jesus, tried to remain faithful in church, trusted God, and took one step at a time—one day at a time.

I still detest Dax and all my other abusers. As hard as it is, however, I choose to forgive them with God's strength and help. The Holy Spirit resides in me, enabling me to maintain a clean heart. His grace is sufficient for me (2 Cor. 12:9) to get through these challenges. When thoughts of anger or bitterness return, I pour my heart out before God. He understands. He knows my innermost being, sustains and uplifts me. He meets me where I am—not only in the good and victorious moments but in the painful and messy ones, as well. I do not and will not have any contact with people who abused me, but I still forgive them and pray that they find redemption and true repentance.

Relationships are a two-way street. Marriage requires effort, dedication, and initiative; love, communication, trust, understanding, honesty, and intimacy go both ways. It cannot be a one-man show. Most importantly, no excuse exists for abuse or domestic violence. Women are not rehabilitation centers to fix broken men. Over the years, I learned the hard way that we must heal, change, work on ourselves, improve, and be happy before bringing someone else into our lives. We need to honor God in our relationships, marriages, and families. If we leave God out of the equation, we are doomed.

Recalling these incidents makes me feel sick to my stomach. I wish I could go back in time and help young Grace out of the horror she endured, remaining trapped in the web of uncertainty caused by that terrible marriage. This life, this journey of mine, has helped me grow, learn, mature, and transform in various ways. It was not always easy. Much pain, heartache, disappointment, loneliness, grief, shame, anger, tears, betrayal, and despair filled my days. I choose to hold on tightly to God and to allow His purposes to be fulfilled in my life.

I believe that some of us are chosen warriors in a complex battle, experiencing things that not everyone can. Through that challenge, the warrior becomes stronger and wiser—more equipped and empowered to fight on behalf of others. We can relate, intercede, understand, empathize, pray, support, and love. We can help others connect to Jesus and have victory over their situations.

As I continue to love and trust God, I know that He will work things out for my good. He always has. My desire is for my story to glorify God and to help others in similar situations. I write in order to spread hope, victory, and courage for me, for you, for future generations. God has restored all that I have lost and given me beauty for ashes.

8
DXB: High Up in the Sky

After the divorce, I spent a month during the summer of 2008 with Pastor Chad and Jennifer in Irving, Texas. Their kindness, patience, and hospitality brought healing, happiness, and peace. I also enjoyed attending services with them at Living Word Global Church. Pastor Chad's sermons were life-changing.

Randomly scrolling the internet one morning, I thought about Emirates, an airline I had flown on as a passenger when I was sixteen. Their service and flight attendants fascinated me. They seemed prestigious, classy, pleasant, and professional. Feeling led of the Lord, I went to the career section and decided to submit an application for the cabin crew (flight attendant) role. God blessed me with people skills, sociability, attention to detail, empathy, the gift of the gab, a nice smile, and a flair for words. I am grateful that all these qualities and His favor have opened doors for me in various places. I would be so lost without God.

My resumé lacked certain requirements and academic qualifications, but I listed a few of my people-related experiences and applied, anyway, using a photo on my phone. It was a bit silly of me, to be honest, but I was bold in trying new things, taking risks, and stepping out of my comfort zone. I felt a bit anxious but soon stopped thinking about it, deciding to leave the rest in God's hands. If the role was meant to be mine, I would get it. Otherwise, I knew God would have something else in store for me. At the end of the month, I returned home to Singapore.

I did not know how my life would unfold. I even considered the possibility of returning to Texas and starting a life there. Having sold my matrimonial flat, I did not have a place of my own and did not want to return to my parents' house. I was grateful when my older brother and sister-in-law opened their door to me for a while. I knew I could not stay there for long and did not want to be a burden. I also did not want to invade the privacy of others. God knew my heart. He understood my challenges, concerns, and frustrations. I needed a way out—a life of my own. I needed the freedom to be myself, make my own decisions, explore life, depend on God, and figure things out.

One day, I decided to log on to my brother's computer and started clearing out junk mail and found an email from Emirates that had arrived a few days earlier. My heart raced. It was an invitation to the Emirates Open Day in Singapore, being held that very day! Surprised and excited, I had only a few hours until it began. Then the panic set in—I did not have the right clothes or any documents printed or the necessary photos. As a result of the divorce, most of my things were still in boxes.

In addition, my parents did not know about this; and working for Emirates would mean relocating to Dubai. My dad would not be pleased with my living abroad on my own. Growing up, I encountered different people who used words like *wild, party girl, loose,* or *mile-high club* when describing female flight attendants—misconceptions that were fueled by ignorance, stereotyping, and closed-mindedness.

Flight attendants do pursue various lifestyles. You get exposed to many things living abroad on your own, traveling the world, earning well, and getting to know people from different nationalities. The job affords freedom, fun, excitement, and adventure. Nonetheless, each individual is different, and lifestyle is all about choices: our value systems, morals, beliefs, backgrounds, and mindsets.

Being a flight attendant also involves hard work, discipline, tact, personality, patience, service excellence, time zones, jet lag, different climates, busy rosters, weird sleep schedules, and odd hours of work. Many flight attendants have families to provide for. They train hard for their role; and apart from customer satisfaction and meal services, they are also responsible for the safety and security of passengers on board.

Seeing this email so last-minute really made me anxious. I had to figure out how to get to the location. I could not think properly but had to act fast. I did not have much cash, and time was of the essence. It was a big step to take and tricky decision to make in a short period of time. I honestly did not know what to do.

Shutting myself in the room alone for a few minutes, I said, "God, I don't know what move to make. I don't know if I should go ahead with this. But I feel all alone. I know I don't belong here in Singapore at this point of my life. I don't even have my own home to live in. So much has happened, and I feel like I am caught in a big mess. I don't even know if I will get this job. If this is meant for me, please let it work out. Come through for me. If this is not part of Your plan, then let me not get this job. And grant me the assurance to know that You will have something better in store for me. Please make a way for me, God."

I dressed quickly and saved my resumé, some school certificates, and a testimonial on a thumb drive—a little concerned about not having a high school completion certificate, since I left school at sixteen to go help in Uganda. I printed documents at a nearby photo studio and had pictures taken.

Time moved quickly. Interviews were being held at a hotel downtown; and I had to be there on time, so my remaining cash went to a taxi. It can feel scary when you have to take risks, step out of your comfort zone, or attempt things you might not be qualified for. But sometimes, you have to be willing to try. Remaining stagnant and complacent can be lethal. In order to experience growth and progress, you sometimes have to embrace change.

Finally arriving at my destination, I entered the hotel and headed to the ballroom where the Open Day was being held. Flabbergasted was how I felt—extremely flabbergasted, uncomfortable, and awkward. I was the only one underdressed! I felt so out of place. I did not fit in. Everyone else was in formal office wear and business suits. Meanwhile, I was barely holding it together without enough money to buy formal wear and many other things I needed. The $10,000 I had received from the sale of the flat had already been used. I gave half to my parents out of love for them; 10 percent went to my tithe; some of it went to my brothers as a gift; and the remainder was used for my much-needed trip to Texas. This Open Day was important to me.

In the opening session, they filtered and selected the people they wanted for the actual interview. I felt uncertain but continued to place my trust in God. The other women looked immaculate with their makeup, business suits, stockings, high heels, and French twist hairstyles. They looked so well-groomed and ready to ace the interview; and there I was, very casual in a short, peach-colored dress and grayish pink sneakers. My really bad hair day had resulted in a messy bun; I wore minimal makeup and big hoop earrings, and I was carrying a Nike bag. By God's grace, I had a clear complexion.

I felt insecure. It was tough, but I was still somehow optimistic. I was determined and held on to hope. Believing that my story was not over yet, I knew God could turn things around.

Two or three hundred people turned up for the Open Day. I stood in line, filled out the required forms, and submitted my documents. They took pictures of me—a face shot and full-length. After everything was done, I returned home; and the waiting period began. If we were selected for the interview, we would get an email or receive a call. If we did not hear from them within a week or so, we did not get selected. I was anxious. I did not want to be disappointed, but I also knew that certain things were beyond my control. I had to patiently trust the process.

A few days later, the Emirates recruiting team informed me that I had been selected for an interview. Phew! What a relief it was! I gave thanks to God for the opportunity. I knew that I could not go through this interview without His help. I want Him in every stage of my life. I may look nice, speak well, and connect with people efficiently; but without God, everything is in vain. All that I am is because of Him. Everything I have is because of Him. Every blessing, talent, skill, attribute, quality, gift, and miracle is due to His goodness and providence. It would be foolish to think that I can do life without Jesus.

The interview was divided into various stages over a period of two weeks. After each session, interviewees quietly approached a big desk that held individual envelopes with each person's name. You opened it discreetly to find a little note, indicating whether or not you were selected to proceed to the next level. It was pretty nerve-wracking. The group size decreased little by little, and I was sad to see new friends leave. I could imagine their disappointment. It also made me nervous about making it to the next stage.

Some interviews were one-to-one sessions; others were held as group discussions. In one, they made me sit next to a huge, full-length window with sunlight shining through while they carefully examined my skin, teeth, and physique. They asked why I thought they should hire me and made me talk about myself. They observed how we interacted in groups and gave us different issues to solve. In one session, many little pieces of paper with different words on them were placed on the ground; and we had to quickly select one, look at the words the other people had, and form the words into sentences that created a scenario or story. The interviewers noted our nonverbal communication, people skills, fluency in English, physical appearance, and mannerisms, as well as how we handled challenging discussions, resolved customer complaints, and demonstrated teamwork.

I enjoyed these sessions and became acquainted with a lot of other people. We got along well and hung out after interviews. It was fun and memorable. I enjoyed how interactive, challenging, and interesting the interviews were. I displayed efficient communication, attention to detail, teamwork, leadership skills, humor, openness, and kindness in each session. I trusted in God, regardless of the outcome. I also expressed my desires and asked for His will to be done.

The group size gradually decreased from a few hundred to just thirty applicants. The last stage was the final interview with a panel of three interviewers. Nervous, I prepared well for that day, dressing presentably and telling myself that I would give it my best. The week before the final stage, a man prepped us for the final interview. He gave us advice and tips on what would be expected, made us do lots of talking, and required us to share our experiences with one another. Many of the applicants were nervous and struggled with public speaking. Some were confident enough to speak but did not know what to say. Some of them did not have much experience in dealing with people and, therefore, were not able to engage in certain topics. Seeing how each person reacted was a learning experience for all of us, indeed. I tried to encourage many of them and wanted everyone to feel valued. Only five or ten people, including me, were now advancing to the final stage.

Each interviewer asked me different questions and wanted me to elaborate on specific incidents. I answered every question to the best of my ability and offered more detail than they expected. Although I was nervous, I remained calm, poised, pleasant, cheerful, and confident in my responses and demeanor. The interviewers responded well, gave their feedback, wished me luck, and told me that I would hear from them if I was selected for the job. The waiting time is usually the hardest, but I knew God had the final say and that my life was in His hands.

The Emirates recruitment team let me know in the next day or so that I was hired for the role! Only two of the thirty candidates—another girl and I—were selected. My heart rejoiced, and my mind was relieved. I gave glory to God, knowing He had come through for me. His favor was upon me, and I was grateful.

The next two weeks were busy. I submitted various new-hire documents, signed my contract, attended medical check-ups, received vaccines, and gave my passport details. I eventually informed my family about the job and that it required me to be based in Dubai, and the sudden news surprised my parents. I guess, despite the uncertainty and worries, they were somehow glad for me. They were probably worried, too; and the reality of my leaving the country was hard for them to digest, especially for my sixteen-year-old brother. I knew they would miss me. I would miss them, too. But absence sometimes makes the heart grow fonder, and the distance does help at times.

Selected candidates usually wait two-to-six months—and sometimes longer—before being flown over to the United Arab Emirates (UAE). During this time, tests are completed, results submitted, and documents processed. Without a place of my own to live in, I knew I was not able to wait a few months; nonetheless, I could not control or manipulate the situation and had to be patient, tell God my needs, trust His timing, and let the process take its course.

We serve a miracle-working God Who knows what we need, when we need it, and how to bring things to pass. "Always ready to help in times of trouble" (Psalm 46:1), He is a God Who exceeds our expectations. Less than a month after being selected for the role, Emirates called to ask if I could relocate to Dubai in one week. I said yes! They sent flight details, the address of my apartment in Dubai, and the dates of my training in the Emirates Aviation College—fully paid for by Emirates. What a blessing!

I purchased suitcases, packed to relocate, spent time with my immediate family, and started saying my goodbyes. Leaving home was sad, but I knew it was necessary. I also knew that we would be in touch, and I could visit them whenever possible.

Getting used to living alone in Dubai, without friends or family, took a few months. I had to get adjusted and find my way around and soon started to make friends during training and flights. Before being cleared to fly, I had to complete several weeks of intense training. We learned safety and emergency procedures, aircraft types, evacuation methods, procedures for crash landing and ditching, restraining unruly passengers, handling various equipment on board, customer service, food and beverage service, and first aid. This training continues for the duration of our career, even after we pass initial training and start flying.

I greatly enjoyed my time with Emirates. Traveling the world, seeing places, meeting new people, earning well, making memories, and staying in beautiful hotels were such a blessing. The job did have its challenges and frustrations; and I worked hard on board and did my best, ensuring excellent service delivery on each flight, practicing integrity, and showing kindness.

Each flight brought a different experience. Some destinations and passenger profiles were nice; some were not. You encounter polite, respectful, humble, and pleasant people, as well as individuals who are rude, arrogant, untidy, and unreasonable. Some flights were quick, fun, and easy; others were long, tiring, and stressful. We learned to manage, work well, and have efficient teamwork, regardless of the situation. I developed a few beautiful friendships along the way; and I still keep in touch with some of them, though we have all gone our separate ways or live in different countries.

I am grateful that God gave me the opportunity to fly with Emirates. I could not have done it on my own. It was His favor that got me through and kept me safe in different climates, time zones, flight durations, and seasons. One day, we were in Germany and another in Japan. We ate dinner in Singapore and had breakfast in Australia or woke up in the UAE and went to bed in the USA. The roster schedule and fast-paced work environment did mess with our sleep cycle and health sometimes, but the overall experience with Emirates was wonderful.

It is the world's largest international airline, flying to 158 destinations in eighty-five countries. Traveling can be very beneficial, educational, and inspiring. It broadens your mindset and changes your perspective on life. I enjoyed working as a flight attendant and liked the lifestyle that came with it. I could financially support myself and also contribute to my parents; and I finally had the space, freedom, independence, and exposure I needed.

Being in Dubai while working with the airline does offer many benefits: free gym memberships, discounts in places of entertainment and leisure, and discounted flight tickets. As with any other job or country, there are always pros and cons. Challenges are part and parcel of life. But on the whole, I have many pleasant memories of working with Emirates. Dubai felt like my second home. I would get a Singapore (SIN) flight on my roster every three to eight months. It takes six hours and forty-five minutes to seven hours to fly from

Dubai to Singapore. I split my thirty days of annual leave into six trips (five days each), which enabled me to travel home to Singapore a bit more and go on short holidays.

During my seven years in Dubai, I was with Emirates for about four years and later worked as a store manager in a flagship location of Destination Maternity in the Dubai Mall, one of the biggest and busiest malls in the city. Dubai is a place that I will always recall with many bittersweet memories.

No matter what comes my way, I can trust that God has a plan for me. I can face tomorrow with hope because God will never forsake me. Like Isaiah 49:15-16 says, "Can a mother forget her nursing child? Can she feel no love for the child she has borne? But even if that were possible, I would not forget you! See, I have written your name on the palms of my hands."

9
Divorce 2: Disappointed but Determined

During my time in the UAE, I met someone I shall call Hadi. We worked for the same company and lived in the same apartment building. Looking back, I am not exactly sure what I saw in Hadi or how I fell for someone like him. At that time, however, I continued to feel the void from my divorce. Dax had caused a lot of damage; and I was trying to heal from the rejection, low self-worth, and betrayal. My standards were low, and I was not able to believe that I deserved better.

I was also eager to have a fresh start in life after all the years of heartache. I wanted to be free and happy. Still new in Dubai, I did not know many people yet and was not intentionally looking for a relationship. As I got to know Hadi, though, he began to pursue me. I wish I had said no and took my time to get to know other people or simply focused on my job as a flight attendant; but his companionship and interest in me made me feel loved, desired, and seen. I did not realize that I was actually filling the deep emptiness in my heart in the wrong way. I began to spend more time with him.

At first, I was happy and enjoyed the activities we did together, hanging out with friends and exploring the UAE. Eventually, we fell in love. Our friends knew about our relationship; and after six to eight months of being together, we informed our families. Within a year, he proposed and put a ring on my finger.

We had good moments and cared about each other. I took the relationship seriously and was committed to making it work. We had different flight schedules and rarely operated any flights together. However, we did go on holidays and also visited our families in Singapore and Tunisia. Our personalities were different, but I always tried to compromise and keep the peace.

With time, I began to notice several red flags. I know that I am not perfect and had my flaws, but I was a caring and attentive partner and put his needs before mine. I also foolishly chose to ignore traits and issues with him. It is a good thing to be patient with people, empathize, and look for the good in others; but this practice does not apply to every person and situation. Not everyone deserves that kind of understanding. Wisdom, discernment, and boundaries are important. Love, communication, respect, loyalty, trust, and honesty are two-way streets. Both parties have to invest in the relationship, take the initiative, and put in the effort. If only one person always shows love, gives, makes adjustments, sacrifices, and ensures that things work, the relationship will fail. The bond will not be a healthy one.

Hadi had his secrets. He had passwords on his laptop, iPad, and both his mobile phones. I had no access to them and could not utilize them. If I mentioned the words *transparency*, *trustworthiness*, or *openness* in our relationship, he would reply that I did not trust him and was overly sensitive. I sensed that he had things to hide but wanted to avoid conflict and tried to show that I trusted him. He was manipulative that way, and it was a major red flag; but I kept thinking

I could fix the situation. I told myself that things would improve with time. I chose to believe that he would be better and wanted to give him the benefit of doubt. I truly cared about him and did not want to give up on him.

Hadi was a workaholic: money-minded and self-centered. I was blinded by love and told myself that he was hardworking, financially stable, and not complacent. True, he may not have been lazy with work, but he was too focused on earning money. His priorities were not in the right place. Hadi was very thrifty but in the wrong ways—he would spend on things that were unnecessary but stinge on important things. He refused to buy a new mop, even if the one we had was almost falling into pieces and covered in rust, instead covering it with tape and forbidding me from buying one. It was really weird. I was not a spendthrift person, but Hadi interfered in my decisions to buy household items. I always remained silent and tried to keep the peace.

No matter what the discussion or argument, I had to be the one to give in and apologize because Hadi considered himself perfect. He put himself before anyone else and was very proud. He had his good qualities, but there were many things wrong about him. He was not a good partner. Our mindsets were different.

I also discovered that Hadi had no integrity, morals, or conscience. I kept filling his life with love, admiration, and appreciation, encouraging him to be the best version of himself. He focused only on more money, freedom, and fun. He lacked good values and honesty.

I still chose to recall the nice times we had, focused on his positive traits, overlooked his flaws, and looked for the good in him. I should have left the relationship sooner but was blinded by love and did not want to give up on him. I believed that people could change for the better if given the right opportunity and love.

Staying in a toxic relationship was unwise. I am not God to change a person. Women are not rehabilitation centers for broken men. Because I had not fully healed, I made the mistake of seeking acceptance, validation, approval, and love from Hadi, when the void in my heart was something that only God could fill. My standards were low, and I could not see that I deserved better. I opened my heart fully to Hadi, who gave me only certain parts of his.

I lacked the courage and self-love to remain alone or to walk away from something unhealthy. Hadi always put himself first and disregarded my needs, based on his moods. If he was upset, he withheld communication and blocked me from any mode of contact; yet I stayed. A superficial person, he always wanted me to look good, asking me to put on makeup every time we went out and commenting on my weight if I decided to eat some bread. He remarked on my skin, clothes, and body parts.

I was, and still am, a beautiful woman. It feels funny when I say something nice about myself. I do not like to compliment myself, but I should. Acknowledging your own strengths and qualities in a humble way is not wrong, especially when you have been put down for so many years. So, yes, I am a beautiful, strong, eloquent, smart, brave, and kind person. "Thank you for making me so wonderfully complex! Your workmanship is marvelous—how well I know it" (Psalm 139:14).

Hadi made me feel self-conscious. I started to dislike parts of me, feeling embarrassed about my body and hiding certain areas. He would love me on some days and break me on others. Now I can see that it was all due to his own insecurities and inferiority complex. He thought too highly of himself; and little by little, he tried to further break my self-esteem. He wanted me to feel like I could not live my life without him and made me feel like he was too good for me. I slowly started to believe him without even realizing it. The sad truth is that people will treat you the way you allow them to treat you.

This relationship had more downs than ups. We still carried on the daily routine of our lives as normal. He started deejaying on the side and spent a lot of time spinning and organizing parties and events. I tried to be as supportive as I could, not wanting him to give up on his dreams and passions. I encouraged him and always boosted his self-esteem.

After four years of dating, we decided to get married. The ceremony took place at the Italian Consulate in Dubai, since Hadi also had an Italian passport. We then flew to Singapore for a wedding dinner with my side of the family, followed by a trip to Tunis to gather with his side of the family and spend some time there before heading back to Dubai. Everything seemed good, and we were happy. I started looking forward to our life together.

The happiness was short-lived. Things began to worsen after we got married. As usual, his moods fluctuated. Some days, he was nice; and on others, he was unpleasant. When he was not busy with flights, he filled his days off with deejay gigs. He started buying and renting out equipment for events and filled our house and car with speakers, lights, cables, smoke machines, dance floors, subwoofers, bubble machines, microphones, stands, and tapes. It was a disaster, and he gave me no say in any of it. Because he was a man and earned much more than I did, he tried to call all the shots. He had a lot of ego and narcissism, and he was proud of it.

He rented out a small storage unit and did not want to spend on a bigger unit, even though he made good money. (I do not know where the money went, but I was aware that he bought some land in Tunisia.) We did not live a rich life; and our simple, small apartment in Dubai began to resemble a dusty, unsightly storage unit, too, which caused me considerable stress and tension. I could not say a word, as he would start a fight with me. I wanted to avoid any kind of quarrel. I think, deep inside, I did not want to lose the relationship. It was a wrong move, but I was not able to see it then.

Sometimes, wanting to keep the peace for the wrong reasons and wrong people will cost you big time. I started feeling stuck and frustrated but showed him love and appreciation. He worked so much and was focused on making more money. He had little rest and became very easily irritable. He was often on his phone, cracked open many cans of beer each day, and became nasty with his words if I had different views or called out his unwise behavior. He was always so tired, agitated, or slightly drunk that we barely had much quality time together. He wanted to work out all the time and insisted that I did, too. Sometimes, he seemed to love me for who I was; and other times, he seemed to suddenly dislike my skin color, body, and parts of me. He watched a lot of pornography and allowed it to mess with reality and true intimacy.

I observed him looking at other women in the gym or at the pool and found email conversations between him and female passengers he tried to befriend. These things hurt me and dampened my confidence. I always felt like I was not good enough. I was afraid to confront him regarding these matters, knowing him to be an unreasonable person. Having a proper discussion with him was not possible. He turned things into a fight and walked out on me.

I did not have energy for the fights. Insecure and emotionally weak, I kept trying to make things work, even though I could see that he was not right for me. I did not want to go through the pain, embarrassment, and stress of another divorce. I kept believing that he would change and that my love could win him over again.

He had left his job with Emirates to work with a different airline; so though we were still in the same country, he was not in Dubai anymore. This situation meant that I did not know his circle of friends there. I had many concerns about what could be happening, especially since he was not that caring toward me any longer; but I continued to trust and affirm him.

No longer a flight attendant, I worked six days a week as a store manager and looked forward to our time together. I tried to dedicate my one day off each week to being with him; instead, he took on extra flights, chose to spin for more gigs, rented equipment out, and helped customers set up for events. Nothing came before him and his money. I kept lying to myself, thinking it was just a phase and that he would realign his priorities in due time.

Eight or nine months after getting married, I was overjoyed and excited to discover that I was pregnant. I had always wanted to be a mother. After failing to conceive during my first marriage and never finding out why, knowing that I was now pregnant made me glad and content. I shared the good news with him when he got home from a flight. He did not seem as excited or emotional as I was—he just said okay, smiled, and told me that he was tired. I convinced myself that he was really exhausted after a long flight.

Over the next few weeks, he slowly started to embrace the pregnancy. He started showing some affection and care, but it would not last for long. From time to time, he would still be rude, unavailable, and easily irritable. Treading carefully around his mood swings was exhausting, and he was never consistent. He also started having anger outbursts toward me and grabbed my hair painfully a few times.

One night, I looked forward to going out for dinner with him. I missed quality time and intimacy and got dressed up, feeling really pretty. When he started having a few cans of beer, I said I was not comfortable with him drinking every day and told him not to drink and drive, as it was dangerous and wrong. I worried about his safety and wanted to protect myself and the baby in my womb. He got angry and canceled our night out, telling me that I could go have sex with the security guard downstairs if I wanted intimacy. He prepared to fall asleep on the couch. Hurt, lonely, and heartbroken, I cried so much that night. I told him not to make me cry, that it was not healthy for a pregnant woman to be so sad and cry. He brought me a plastic container and told me to hold it under myself just in case I miscarried, mocked me, and soon fell asleep.

Many nights and days filled with silent tears. I continued working and spent a lot of time on my feet, due to my job. He would not let me resign, wanting me to pay half of every bill and the rent. He made two to three times more than what I earned, yet he was still calculative. Even on days I did not feel comfortable driving to work, he would forbid me from taking a taxi because it was a waste of money. He would drive me sometimes but reached the point of being too busy. He did not seem to care about the well-being of the baby and me. We carried on with life as normal, and I tried to pretend that everything was okay. I was carrying his child and wanted to make the marriage work.

As the months went by, we started to prepare for the arrival of the baby. The apartment was small, but he did not think we should move. Together, we bought things for the baby and stocked up on the necessities. I decided to give birth in Singapore; so I could have the help of my mom and be around family—especially since Hadi would be busy, and we did not have family in Dubai. I did not want his mom around, due to the language barrier; and I knew I would feel comfortable being around my mom after childbirth.

Thankfully, Hadi agreed. He arranged for me to have a private, single-bed room in the hospital, to which my father also contributed. Everything seemed to be going well, and I was excited about the baby. I did not mind having a baby boy or girl; the most important thing was for the baby to be healthy. I did feel in my heart that it would be a girl, and I preferred to have a baby girl as my firstborn. It was just something that I liked; but ultimately, I left the decision to God. Guess what? I was pregnant with a baby girl! When I was six months along, we took a vacation to Thailand. It was nice. I felt so beautiful and feminine being pregnant.

I applied for maternity leave and told Hadi I wanted to resign after giving birth, since I wanted to take care of the baby myself. At least for the first year of her life, I wanted to be present—to breastfeed and be dedicated to raising the child. Hadi was not pleased. His idea was for me to keep earning, to pay the bills, and to leave the baby with a nanny. I disagreed and stood my ground. He was not happy with the idea but played it cool since I had not yet resigned.

I flew home to Singapore alone about a month before my due date, following the flying regulations and carrying my doctor's letter with me. Being home in Singapore was nice. Everyone was kinder to me because I was pregnant. I was excited about having the baby and getting all her cute, little clothes ready.

At thirty-seven weeks, I had to be induced rather suddenly. Hadi took urgent leave and arrived the day I was going into labor. I gave birth on August 22, 2014, at 10:28 a.m. Singapore time. I named my little beauty Rania and cried as I held my precious, little girl in my hands—my baby, my beautiful daughter. Hadi was happy to see her, too. He flew back to the UAE two days later, needing to return to work and wanting to get the apartment ready.

I spent another few months in Singapore. The first month was the confinement period for Rania and me, which is common in Asian culture. Mothers stay at home with their newborns. This period is accompanied with confinement drinks—meal options that include specific ingredients and herbs to help boost immunity, nourish the body, replenish energy, increase strength, and enhance breast milk supply. As Asians, we also had postpartum massages and belly wraps (or belly binding), which support the abdominal muscles and help the uterus contract. We also went to doctor's appointments. My mom took a month of leave from work to help me, for which I am so grateful. Having her around was really helpful for me.

I had to sort documents and apply for Rania's passport, so we could travel back to Dubai. During this time, I tendered my resignation. My operations manager was a really good boss—kind, supportive, honest, and diligent. He acknowledged my hard work and skills and offered me the role of an area manager, which would obviously come with a pay raise. I politely declined and told him that I wanted to focus on my baby. He understood and helped arrange my resignation.

Before I arrived from Singapore with baby Rania, Hadi changed the apartment door's locks without telling me. One day, the fire alarm in the building went off, and I realized that my keys did not work. Hadi was on a layover. I tried to call and text him, but he did not respond. When he finally answered the phone after a long time, he said it was not a big deal and that I should stop being so dramatic—that I was disturbing his peace by calling him. I tried explaining the danger of not being able to leave the apartment, but he replied that it was probably just a false alarm.

Hearing that made me angry. We did not know for sure if it was a false alarm or if there was an actual fire. I was alone in the apartment with Rania, and Hadi was going to return home three days later. How was I supposed to step out of the apartment with Rania to take a walk and have fresh air? How was I supposed to get groceries? What if Rania suddenly became unwell, and I had to take her to the hospital? He did not care. He soon hung up on me and blocked my number. He was negligent, irresponsible, and did not prioritize our well-being. It made me really sad and disappointed. I cried out to God, heartbroken.

When he entered the apartment three days later, he immediately asked if the baby and I had died in the fire and if the apartment had burned down. Laughing, he called me dramatic and passed the new set of keys to me, saying that I liked to overreact.

I breastfed Rania and took good care of her. Hadi was rarely home; and even when he was, he was not approachable or helpful. He checked to see if the house was dusty and controlled everything I did. Because I was no longer working, he gave me an allowance; but it was not sufficient to cover all my needs. He started asking me for receipts to track my spending. He asked when I would lose the baby weight and get back in shape, threatening to see other women if I did not get fit again. My body was still tender, raw, and tired from childbirth, sleepless nights, and breastfeeding Rania; but Hadi did not care. He made me feel self-conscious and offered no room for intimacy, sleeping on the couch in the living room because he did not want the baby's cry to disturb his sleep.

It felt like a nightmare. On days that he was home after a flight or after his multiple events and meetings, I had to stay inside the bedroom with the baby and not come out, so he could sleep. I felt trapped and alone. I was not free to move around or enjoy motherhood. He expected me to keep Rania quiet and said that she should not cry when he was sleeping. His demands became more ridiculous with time. It was stressful and overwhelming.

I spent many days and nights alone and had to manage Rania's care on my own. Hadi was selfish and said that he came before Rania, myself, or anyone else. He was number one—his very words. Nothing else came before him. He barely carried Rania or spent any time with her. It broke my heart. My poor baby Rania did not deserve such treatment. The reality was hard to digest.

Whenever he felt like it, he blocked me on his phone to prevent contact. I am so grateful that I could turn to God for strength, wisdom, patience, hope, and love. Protecting, loving, and caring for

Rania were my priorities; and I loved every moment with her. Though some days were tough, I was so happy to be her mommy. She was my precious gift from God.

Meanwhile, Hadi was turning into something horrible, and it tore me apart. I loved and cared about him and wanted to be a good wife and mother, but life with him became more miserable with each passing day. We started speaking less, since he was hardly home or not in a good mood. Annoyed at the sight of me, he was constantly on his phone and paid no attention to cute, little Rania. There was no communication, connection, intimacy, or transparency between us. When I tried to reach out to him or salvage things, his poor attitude and indifference got in the way. It hurt me to know that he did not care about us. He failed Rania as a father. I felt embarrassed that things had turned out this way—rejected, betrayed, and unappreciated. I could not understand why he did not cherish our marriage and child. It made me sad to know that he did not want to embrace a beautiful family life.

He became more distant. Once, when he left his laptop open and went to the bathroom, I looked through the browsing history and discovered that he had signed into websites for swingers. He had also minimized a page on social escort sites in Frankfurt that explained how to obtain sex services in your hotel room. It made me sick to my stomach, knowing that he was actually operating as a flight attendant on a flight to Frankfurt the next day.

My heart was in so much pain, but I remained silent to avoid trouble at home. I wanted to keep Rania safe and well. I wanted a happy family life. I wanted to love and be loved in return. It is truly hurtful and devastating when your husband does not love, appreciate, and desire you anymore, especially when you have just brought his child into this world.

One afternoon, I realized that my breast pump bag had been emptied. All the milk bottles, tubes, pumps, and other accessories were removed and placed carelessly on a shelf in the house with other random items. Wires, duct tape, and spare tools now occupied the bag. Milk pumping items needed to be sterilized and kept really clean, so I felt upset. I was very careful with matters concerning Rania. I took good care of her things, and hygiene was essential. Her health and safety were important to me. I also did not want to lose any part of the breast pump kit.

I asked Hadi why his items were in my breast pump bag. He did not respond and continued using his laptop. I asked again, telling him not to use the breast pump bag for other things. He became agitated and told me to shut up. I then politely told him that I was going to remove his things and put the breast pump kit back inside its dedicated bag. Hadi looked at me angrily and told me not to touch his stuff. I replied that it was my breast pump bag, which was meant for Rania, and proceeded to remove his things carefully, placing them on the couch next to him.

Suddenly, Hadi threw a 1.5-liter bottle of mineral water at me. It hit me hard on the chest, which was already sore and tender from nursing the baby. He got up and began to punch me continuously, pushing me until my back hit the apartment door. He punched my face a few times and walked away. I was in so much physical and emotional pain. Holding back tears, I kept my eyes fixed on Rania, who was lying on the bed, crying for milk. My focus was on monitoring that she would not roll off the bed or be left hungry. I also wanted to ensure that Hadi would not lay a hand on her. He was unstable and angry. Thankfully, he did not hurt her.

Once he walked away from me, I quickly went into the room and held Rania in my arms, whispering, "Mommy will never let anyone hurt you," and nursed her as she gazed into my eyes. My whole body was sore and throbbing from the pain, and my heart was broken. Due to the punches, I would not be able to chew for a few days; and my face was really sore. But seeing Rania and holding her close to me made me forget my worries. I cried out to God silently and asked Him for strength and wisdom to deliver me from this turmoil. I prayed for protection. I did not know what to do. I felt unsafe in the apartment with Hadi and worried about Rania.

I wanted to do the right thing; but knowing Hadi did not care about us, I did not know what it was. We were married and living in Dubai with no other family around. I was taking care of a little baby and no longer employed. It was a tricky situation. I did not want to give up on the marriage; I still cared about him. At the same time, I did not condone the way he was treating Rania and me. I did not want to be caught up in another abusive marriage, exposing Rania to domestic violence or an unstable environment; I wanted to raise her in a home that is wholesome, healthy, and filled with love. Unable to make a decision, I needed God to come through for me. I was confused, lonely, afraid, and depressed.

Through it all, my priority was Rania. Her safety, comfort, and health were of extreme importance. For the next two days, Hadi barely spent time at home, coming and going at odd hours. When he was home, he would not speak to me or tend to Rania. At night, he slept on the couch. I remained in the room with Rania the entire day and sneaked out to the kitchen just to grab a bite of whatever I could find. At bedtime, I would lock the room door.

I started having fearful thoughts that Hadi might come in at night and stab Rania and me with a knife in order to get rid of us. I imagined him killing me and leaving Rania in Tunisia for his mother to raise, while he carried on with his foolish lifestyle. All kinds of thoughts and fears filled my mind. I did not want anyone to separate Rania and me.

I cried each night, feeling lost. I was also tired from taking care of Rania all by myself, even though I loved her and would do anything for her. I asked God to make a way for me—for Hadi to have a change of heart and the situation to improve. Deep inside my heart, though, I no longer felt secure, happy, or safe. The apartment was no longer a home or a place of peace.

Two days after the incident, Hadi told me he did not love me anymore and asked me to get out of the apartment. "Take it and leave!" he demanded—the *it* referring to my precious baby, Rania. It felt like my world had come tumbling down. Later, I could see that it was a blessing in disguise; but at the time, it was too painful to understand and too devastating to go through.

After he ordered me to take Rania and get out, he said he could forbid me from going if he wanted. He could withhold our passports and stop me from leaving the country, since he was a man and an Arab. It was his right, and no one would stop him. If necessary, he could tell the police I was a prostitute who refused to leave. He could do as he pleased. My leaving was not my personal choice but his decision to kick me out. He said all these things to show me that he was in charge and that he did not want me or the baby.

I did not argue with him; neither was I rude or angry. I calmly responded that I would leave with Rania as he requested.

"You are not blonde with blue eyes," he sneered. "Look at you. No man would ever want you. You are dark, and you are nothing without me. You will be divorced with a baby, and no man will want you. I will also not respond to any notice of divorce. I will not contribute financially in any way. I will have nothing to do with you. You will suffer without me."

His words cut deeply; but I remained silent and walked away, knowing that plunging into sadness and heartbreak was not the solution right now. I had to be strong and focused. I was Rania's mommy and wanted to do everything necessary to give her a good and happy life.

I wanted to raise her well and fill her life with love. I wanted to enjoy every moment with her and be the best mother possible. I wanted to raise her in God's way and instill good values and morals in her life. She was God's beautiful gift to me. I also knew that God was in control. He was still upon the throne. My life was in His hands. I knew that He would come through for me and "make the crooked places straight" (Isa. 45:2 KJV). I did not know what the future would hold, but I had faith that my future was in the loving hands of my heavenly Father. Though I was afraid and uncertain, I could move forward with hope. I was grateful that Rania was safe with me.

The next day, six-month-old Rania and I flew back home to Singapore. Hadi made it difficult to access my belongings. A dear friend who also lived in Dubai tried to help me retrieve some of my personal things and baby items; but Hadi made it impossible for him, too, so I left everything behind: the apartment, my car, clothes, shoes, bags, documents, accessories, lingerie, toiletries, Rania's cot, baby products, and so many other items. But I had the most precious and valuable possession with me—my Rania.

Returning home to Singapore and starting from scratch was not easy. I could foresee the challenges ahead but was really happy for the ability to live my life peacefully with Rania and to raise her in a safe, healthy environment, even though I missed Dubai. It was also comforting to know that my family was around. I stayed with my parents and younger brother, and everyone had to make adjustments to living together in the small apartment. I appreciate my parents and all their help. They are good grandparents. Rania enjoyed having all of them around.

I stayed home with Rania for the first year of her life. It was a delicate stage, and I wanted to take good care of her without missing any special milestones. I witnessed her first smile, word, step, and other progressions. I am truly thankful that I was able to breastfeed Rania for two-and-a-half years. I exclusively breastfed her for the first six months of her life. After that, I started introducing her to solids (mashed, blended, or soft food). Breast milk was still her primary source of food and nourishment. Like they say, food before one is just for fun! After her sixth month, I started to introduce her to small amounts of water when needed, in addition to my breast milk. When Rania turned one, I started giving her three meals a day, and breast milk became secondary. Her healthy meals were a priority; and she nursed on the side and on demand whenever she was hungry, sleepy, upset, or simply needed comfort.

At the age of one, I introduced her to fresh cow's milk in a sippy cup. I placed her in infant care (daycare) when she was fifteen months old. It made me really sad, but I did not have a choice; I needed to financially support the both of us. I still continued to nurse her early in the morning before going to work and in the evening, once we got home. Breastfeeding helped us bond further, and I cherished every second of it. It did get very tiring, overwhelming, and challenging at times; but I am so glad I could breastfeed her.

I remained single and did not want to jump into another relationship. I needed to heal and get better, and I wanted to dedicate my time to Rania and ensure that she was well-loved. Single motherhood brings emotional, mental, and physical challenges. It took a lot of adjustment, sacrifice, patience, endurance, love, and gratitude. I rarely ever went out alone, hung out with friends, or fostered healthy female friendships, since there was no one to babysit Rania, especially in the evenings or weekends. Even a single mom needs good friends, girl time, and some space to feel like herself again. Having a healthy mind and heart is essential in parenting, especially when you are a single parent.

My parents were gracious in opening their home to us and were helpful in many ways, but I did not get help in the ways that I specifically needed. They were not comfortable with my going out or meeting people and made me bring Rania along or expressed their discontent if I left her with them for just a few hours. My father still tried to impose his control in some ways; and because I was living under their roof, he required me to comply. My father's mindset and mother's passive behavior caused me some sadness and frustration. They are good people, and I love them dearly! But their lack of understanding made it mentally stressful at times, especially after everything I had been through. My immediate family offered no emotional or moral support, and I received no expression of emotions or physical affection. I felt like no one truly understood how I felt or respected my decisions.

But God knew my heart, struggles, and circumstances. I respect and care about my parents. I love my family. I know they love Rania and me, too. Sadly, I have never been able to truly just be myself with them. Despite our differences, I try to treasure every moment with them and focus on the things that unite us. Now, being ninety-two hundred miles apart, we keep in touch with each other as often as we can through text messages or video calls and try to visit each other once or twice a year. Sometimes, distance does help.

Life continued normally in Singapore. Raising Rania was a joy; I adored her wholeheartedly. I hung on to Jesus and never lost faith. God kept me going. I am thankful for His strength. I am also thankful that my family showed lots of love to Rania. I lived one day at a time, believing God would come through for me. In my waiting, God was working.

Although Rania's biological father was not in her life, I did everything I could to meet all her needs. She had me, and I had her. We had family to turn to, and God was looking out for us. I took one step at a time and faced challenges one at a time. I lived within my means and made choices wisely. As Rania grew older, she saw me as both mommy and daddy. I was like her superhero combo. She brought so much love, joy, and fulfilment into my life. I was glad that she could grow up around her grandparents, who pampered her so much.

I knew that my story was not over yet. God had a plan for me and a purpose for Rania's life. I chose to trust God and kept my eyes on Him. It was not always a smooth ride, but I had hope in my heart that better days would come with new beginnings and beautiful adventures. "'For I know the plans I have for you,' says the Lord. 'They are plans for good and not for disaster, to give you a future and a hope'" (Jer. 29:11).

10
Mon Québécois: Coup de Foudre

Time goes by quickly. How do kids grow up so fast? I love every stage of Rania's life, but I do miss how little she was. She was getting taller and bigger and would soon outgrow my lap; but she will never outgrow my arms, heart, and mind. It is a great reminder for me to live one day at a time and to cherish every single moment with my precious Rania! No matter how old she gets, she will always be my baby.

It was January 2020, and Rania would turn six in August. Five years had already gone by since I had returned from Dubai, and I felt like it was time for me to find someone to share my life with—a meaningful companionship and committed relationship that would hopefully turn into marriage. I never stopped believing in true love. I know that Jesus was and is my first Love, and there is no love greater than His. I also believed there was someone out there who was meant for me. Despite my challenging past and two painful divorces, I still believed in love and marriage.

Love and marriage are beautiful and sacred. Yes, there will be challenging days and tedious routines; but when Jesus is part of the story, you get through every situation unitedly and efficiently as one. Intimacy, communication, honesty, loyalty, commitment, and understanding hold you together. God's love keeps you strong.

I had never been with a man who truly loved and prioritized me and did not want to let my past hurts and painful experiences hinder me from the good things ahead. I knew there would be someone out there who loves like I do; who desires true intimacy and romance the same way; who would put in effort, take initiative, and commit wholeheartedly. I asked God to bring me a man who would love me as much as I loved him or maybe even love me more. I knew it was possible, especially for my miracle-working God, my loving Father Who wants the best for me. I just wanted to find true love and to connect with my soulmate with whom I could share my life and love.

I had been out of the dating scene for a long time, and meeting anyone sincere and suitable was hard because I was always at home or work and had no proper opportunity to meet men or have good male friendships. When I was out, Rania was always with me. I knew that not every man would be comfortable with dating a single mother. If I did get to know a man (which was not common), he was either not the right person, or we were on different wavelengths. It was frustrating. Some men desired only the sexual aspect, wanting me only for the way I looked with no interest in pursuing something deeper. I tried to avoid them. I did not want anything shallow or superficial, and I did not want people to waste my time. Nobody wants to get hurt, rejected, or heartbroken.

Though there is so much good around us, I also know that this world can be a scary and unpredictable place. Rania's well-being and safety were still of utmost importance; so while I was looking for love and companionship, I did not want to be a selfish or irresponsible mom. You hear about so many cases of child abuse in the news. I worried about how to let a man into my life and allow him to be a part of Rania's, too. Afraid of someone harming one of us or of ending up in the wrong hands, I wanted to stay alive and healthy for Rania and feared being separated from her. Trusting anyone was a struggle for me, as I had been betrayed by people I trusted and loved in the past.

The abuse, trauma, and pain I experienced brought fear, paranoia, anxiety, and weariness. I took my concerns before God and asked Him for wisdom, protection, patience, boldness, and favor. His peace needed to flood my heart. I had to learn how to trust people again, how to respect myself without compromising good standards, and how to love myself and honor my body. I had to learn how to see myself through God's eyes and remember what His Word says about me. I needed to recognize the red flags and unhealthy patterns in people and to practice setting boundaries. I had to rest in God's unfailing love and be secure in Christ. I had to learn to exercise wisdom, discernment, and patience.

Trusting in God's sovereignty and faithfulness—choosing faith over fear—was a daily decision. I could not be too hard on myself for survival patterns I picked up during the abuse, and I practiced making positive changes along the way. If I started dating a good man, my eventual goal would be building a life with marriage and family. It would also be nice for Rania to have a father who loved her as his own, who loved me deeply, and who made God the center of our lives. I was not sure how any of this was going to happen.

The devil will try to attack the battleground of the mind; and we have to stay on guard, fill our minds with God's Word, and find rest in His presence. Despair and hopelessness can sneak up on you when you are feeling weary and heavy-hearted; and the sudden suicidal thoughts that had come to me at times were frightening, as I did not see them coming. I knew that even in my moment of pain and darkness, God was there with me, and His plan for me is life—a blessed life. His plans for me are good.

After a few years of single parenting, I shared my feelings of occasional loneliness, overwhelm, and depression with my mother, revealing that I had experienced suicidal thoughts one night. I talked about thinking of ending my life, so I would not be a burden to anyone, while at the same time never wanting to leave my Rania alone in this world and desiring to set a good example for her and teach her courage, hope, and resilience through my own example. Wanting to be present in every stage of my daughter's life and knowing my life belonged to God, I tried to hold on to faith, hope, and courage; but I was mentally and emotionally drained.

My mother seemed troubled to hear these things but said nothing. Although I knew she would pray for me, some words of comfort and a hug would have been really helpful. With hesitation, she finally agreed to babysit Rania one evening a month for four or five hours.

My parents were worried about me and cared about Rania. Though Rania was already in bed on those evenings and I was a grown adult, they still called or texted when it was past 10 p.m., asking where I was—a common practice in Asia. Because I was single and female, my father always felt the need to have an input in my life. I love him and know that he wants the best for us all. He cares about the family and is a good grandfather. But many times, his best was not always my best. Speaking my mind, making a stand, and raising concerns while still trying to be respectful, loving, and kind was complicated.

My father would often say, "Conduct yourself. As long as you are under my roof, you listen to what I say." As an adult, that sounded condescending to me each time.

My father did not want me to struggle with a failed relationship again; but his control, lack of understanding, and closed-mindedness had never really helped. It did not help our father-daughter relationship for so many years. Wanting me to remain single and focus on Rania, he would make me feel like I was doing something sinful, like I was an irresponsible mother and would give him a bad name. He always considered worst-case scenarios. It was suffocating. As a result, I was stressed and could not fully enjoy myself. I wanted to please my parents but also needed to do what was good for me.

How was I supposed to develop strong female friendships in person? How would I establish anything meaningful and serious with a man if I were able to socialize without Rania for only a few hours, one evening a month? The man would eventually get bored, lose interest, or not be able to feel any connection with me. We would not have the time and space to know each other on a deeper level. How would I dress beautifully and go for dinners, watch a movie, talk on the phone, plan dates, come home with flowers, or even introduce him to my family?

I had to hide everything, if there was anything at all. It was tough and awkward. I felt uncomfortable going on dates. No one at home understood my feelings, desires, frustrations, and needs. I tried to express my feelings, but everything seemed really complicated. All I wanted was a meaningful connection with a good man.

Still, I am grateful for my parents' care toward Rania and me. They opened their door to us when we were in need and showered Rania with things she needed. We had a roof over our heads and food on the table. Bills were paid, and we were safe. I am thankful for everything. In all my adult life, whenever I was financially stable or successful, I have always found ways to contribute to my parents regularly. My desire is to be blessed so that I can be a great blessing to my parents and help others in need.

Juggling work and single motherhood was also a challenge. I was tired. I could not afford to go on frequent dates, buy pretty clothes, get my hair and nails done, or pay for meals. Apart from missing Rania, going out on my own was uncomfortable. Feeling like I was doing something wrong, I tried to avoid my father as much as possible, in order to avoid awkward conversations, especially if I wanted to go on a date (which was rare). I wished I could talk to him about anything, be open, and feel free. Unfortunately, it was not possible. It was easier for me to share more things with my mother, but she usually did not have much of a say.

I had a few close friends and cousins to whom I could turn through text messages, voice recordings, and occasional phone calls when the challenges of coping with the pain of divorce and single parenting became difficult. I am grateful for them, especially since I had no room or liberty to bare my soul in front of my family.

God saw my pain and frustrations and that of my parents. My situation was not a surprise to God. Even in the midst of my challenging circumstance, I could turn to Him. I may not get my response instantly, and change may not happen straight away; but I could cry out to God, and He would hear me. Nothing was impossible for my miracle-working God, my loving Father. In His own time, He makes all things beautiful and gives us the best when we learn to fully surrender and trust Him. I held on to hope and faith and remained honest and open before God. He would come through for me. He had more for me, more for Rania. I believed in the power of prayer.

I poured my heart out before God, asking Him to help me be more patient and to grant His strength and grace. I asked for His Divine favor and intervention. And though I knew He would bring the right person to me in His own special way, I took my doubts and unbelief before Him. I had to dwell on what was good, noble, pure, and true (Phil. 4:8). I did not want to give up or lose hope. God could turn my life around. He could bring me my life partner in His own beautiful and miraculous way.

I decided to tell God what I desired. He already knew, since no thought or emotion is hidden from Him; but I put it into words, literally writing it down. As I sought after God in obedience, waiting, trusting, openness, vulnerability, and surrender, I knew He would grant my desires as my heart aligned with His. He would fulfill His plans in my life as I chose to walk in His will.

Sitting in the presence of my Heavenly Father, I read out the little checklist and told Him I would be happy with whomever He brought into my life, as long as the man truly loved Rania and me. I also mentioned certain preferences and desires. I mean, why not? He is my Father, my Creator. I am His daughter. I could tell Him anything. God knew that no request stemmed from a bad place. I asked for His will to be accomplished in my life and prayed that He would navigate my journey and direct my steps.

As time went by, God slowly removed people, friends, and relatives from my life who were not good or healthy for me. It was hard to understand at first, but I saw it in due time. He shut doors, realigned my steps, rerouted my journey, removed certain jobs, canceled plans, and helped me get on the right track headed toward my man. In His mercy, He turned my mistakes around and worked things out for my good.

Still lacking a way to interact with men in person, I remembered an online platform that would definitely not have been my choice if I were able to meet people another way; so I approached the new method with caution. Many people would be on that site to hook up with no strings attached; scammers could hope to empty your bank account; other people just wanted sex. But I believed that if I were on that platform with a right mindset and for a right reason, I could find someone who shared the same views. I asked God to help me tread carefully though and choose wisely, not wanting to make decisions out of loneliness or desperation.

I soon started chatting with three or four men, just to find out more about them. Not everyone would suit me, and I would not be a good choice for some men. I tried to be as open as possible, but it was quite frustrating—I had been out of the dating scene for a long time and really had no patience to do all of this. Some men were really shallow and irritating; some were decent and tried to see if we could meet; some were scammers.

Opening up to someone all over again was exhausting. I did not share too much of my past but did offer important details, so they knew what to expect. I made it clear that I was not looking for casual sex, indicating that I wanted something deeper and more meaningful. The babysitting schedule with my parents prevented me from meeting some of them, which was probably a good thing.

As it turned out, I went on only two dates: the first with a football coach from Argentina who lived in Singapore and the other a man from Spain who was the vice president of a company in Singapore. One date worked out better than the other, and we decided to meet again. He seemed really sweet, kind, respectful, and very much interested in me; but I was busy with Rania and work. He too got busy with work, and our chats were slow.

During that time, I started chatting with someone new I came across on the platform. He did not live in Singapore but was passing through. I did not see the need or the importance of communicating with someone with whom I could not really build something in person, although he was nice to chat with. As the days passed, we shared our life experiences; and he was inspired by my story.

He did not seem to mind that I was a single mother; rather, he admired my dedication and told me how strong I was. We shared similar interests in traveling, and I told him about my experiences as a flight attendant with Emirates. I also shared a few details about my challenging past. He showed a lot of interest and told me he wished we lived in the same country, so he could get to know me better and maybe even date me. The conversations made me smile. I was still slightly hesitant to meet someone who was just passing through; and planning anything was hard with my limited time, particularly since my mom may not agree to babysit.

The firefighter's name was Joel Gagnon, and he was one year and nine months older than me. Well, I did tell God that I wanted a man in uniform! I was pleased to know that Joel was a firefighter—how heroic and brave. A French-Canadian, or Québécois like the locals in Montreal say, he spoke both French and English. Tall and handsome, polite and respectful, he had traveled to Vietnam, Thailand, Myanmar, and Malaysia and was currently backpacking through Asia, planning to explore Singapore before heading to the Philippines and then returning to his home in Montreal. All of this was rather appealing to me.

As we kept chatting, Joel asked if I could make time to meet him while he was in Singapore. I replied that it might be rather difficult between working and looking after Rania. Without a babysitter, it would be hard for us to go on a date. I reminded him that he was just passing through Singapore and might meet more people while backpacking around the world, so I did not see the point of our meeting. He persisted and said that, even if it were just for two or three hours in the morning, he would love to meet me for a coffee. I could even bring little Rania along.

I was not too sure but said I would try. He often occupied my thoughts, and an eagerness to meet him started to develop. I was curious to see him in person and get to know him. How could I forego the opportunity to meet a nice guy with a nice personality? He was cute, too! I told myself that anything is possible; you just never know. With God, even the impossible becomes possible. I decided to see how things unfolded from there.

When Joel arrived in Singapore, I told him that I could try to meet him during the daytime. Sending Rania to kindergarten, I left for our

11 a.m. appointment the day after he arrived. I could stay until 5:30, when I had to go get Rania. I felt nervous, shy, and excited at the same time. We met at Paya Lebar in the east region of Singapore, ending up on different sides of the mall and train station and had to text each other. I was wearing an elegant navy blue dress with white flowers on it and carried a black handbag. The straps on my black heels kept coming off as I walked. We found each other, said hi, and did the little kiss greeting on the cheek, happy to finally have met in person.

It was love at first sight. We did not reveal it to each other straight away; but a few weeks later, he told me that it was *coup de foudre* when he first saw me, explaining that it is a French term that refers to an unforeseen event, like a sudden bolt of lightning or love at first sight. I felt the same.

I really enjoy Thai cuisine and wanted to share the experience with Joel. The afternoon was beautiful. While having a delicious lunch, we had a wonderful conversation, too. I talked a lot, of course, and Joel was intrigued and listened intently. We spoke about life, love, family, and traveling. The more we spoke, the more we felt the connection grow. We then proceeded to have coffee and a local dessert. I introduced him to durian fruit. We had a lovely time.

Soon, it was 5:30, and I had to leave. I did not want to be late in getting my precious girl from school. She was still my priority. We said our goodbyes, not knowing if we would see each other again. No promises were made, though we were hopeful. Joel had only a few more days in Singapore; and I said that I would see if my mother could babysit one night, so we could go for dinner.

Knowing I could not openly tell my parents everything, I had to lie to my mom, telling her a close female friend was coming to visit me from overseas. She seemed hesitant. She would be tired after work, and my dad would not be pleased when he found out. My heart sank. I did not want the decisions of my parents to ruin my opportunities or this challenging situation to hinder me from getting to know Joel. I am not the kind of daughter who would take advantage of my parents, nor am I an irresponsible mother; but seeing Joel was important to me.

I asked again if my mother could please help me by watching Rania for a few hours one night. She finally agreed with reluctance. I knew it would not be difficult. Rania was almost six years old. She was not hard to handle and could do some age-appropriate tasks herself. After finishing school by 6:00 p.m. that evening, she would be in bed by 9:00 p.m. All she would need was dinner, some looking after, and some love. I was glad that my mom agreed.

We got together again in the afternoon just two days after our first meeting, exploring Singapore a bit and heading to a Mexican restaurant for dinner. We took a walk down Haji Lane and had a drink. The chemistry was building, and romance was in the air. The physical attraction was mutual. We bonded over our conversations and loved everything about each other. Joel was kind-hearted. I felt comfortable and safe around him. Spending time with him made me happy.

We briefly held hands that day and shared our first kiss. He was leaving for the Philippines in two days. Saying goodbye was sad because I was afraid that it would all be over. He planned to backpack through the Philippines and attend a friend's wedding on another island before heading back to work and life in Montreal. We were unsure of where our situation would lead, with me in Singapore and him in Montreal. It was hard to think about pursuing anything. How were we going to do this—that is, if *this* were even going to happen? But I am someone who embraces challenges; and passionate when it comes to love, I would not give up so easily.

Thankfully, Joel is the same. We were open to seeing where things would lead. He said he would try to come back and see me again if he could. I held on to his words and prayerfully hoped for the best.

We kept in touch while he was in the Philippines. I felt a bit uncertain and worried that he might forget me completely and move on. At the same time, I knew that we had met only twice; so I should not expect anything serious. I was also surprised at myself for kissing him so soon; I was usually reserved and took my time. But my heart had grown fond of him, and I wanted to see him again.

Then the pandemic hit, catching the whole world by surprise. Schools and offices closed. Events, plans, and flights were getting canceled. Airports were shutting down, and borders were closing across the globe. The COVID-19 virus began to spread throughout the world, and countries started to implement extreme safety measures.

Joel had to find a way back to Montreal before he got stranded in the Philippines. Flight cancellations resulted in crowded airports, and poor network connections kept him refreshing the page on his device repeatedly. He finally found one seat available on a flight to Singapore and quickly grabbed that ticket. He was so tense that I felt stressed chatting with him during this period because we knew that time was of the essence. Had he not made it back to Singapore on his way home, who knows when we would have met again? Our lives may have taken different paths. I am so grateful God led Joel back to my country, back to me.

He decided to stay for a few weeks. We met every single weekday after I sent Rania to school and bonded as we got to know each other from 10 a.m. to 6 p.m. It was like a crash course! During this period, only twice did I manage to spend time with Joel until night (not overnight). My mom helped me babysit, if not too willingly, but I was grateful. During these few weeks in March 2020, we fell in love, verbally expressing our feelings for each other and knowing we would make this work. We deleted the dating app from our phones and never looked back. I was on that app for two months. I am glad I found Joel—a pandemic love story, indeed!

During our last evening together, we had a beautiful time at Mr. Stork, a gorgeous rooftop bar at the amazing Andaz Singapore. It was on the thirty-ninth floor and offered a really nice view of the city. We had light bites and some cocktails. It was such a romantic setting, and being there together felt really nice. We were in love, and we each knew that we had found The One.

Joel was to leave Singapore the next morning, and saying goodbye was hard. I introduced him to Rania for the first time that day. Although I was usually very protective of her and would not randomly introduce her to men, I felt strangely safe, comfortable, and secure around Joel. My nerves were not acting up. I was not getting anxious and fearful. My heart felt at peace. All of these feelings confirmed my love for him. Not knowing this good friend of mine (as I described him to her), Rania was shy. Joel was very kind and sweet to Rania. We took her to a pasta place for lunch and still have a picture from that day—such a cute and precious moment.

After so many years of being with the wrong ones, so many years of abuse, and quite a few years of being single, I had finally found a high-value man of character with good values and morals who respected and loved me. A big-hearted, responsible, hardworking man, he kept his word. I was truly grateful to have met Joel. I know he valued me greatly, too. What a blessing!

I could not bear to see him go. Singapore and Canada had closed their borders to incoming visitors, and we knew we may not see each other for a long time. I told him that long-distance relationships are not for everyone; and he needed to let me know if he had doubts, so we did not hurt each other or waste each other's time. Saying yes to me meant saying it to Rania; he would be the only father she ever knew and the only father she ever loved. But if he said yes to us, I would faithfully love him and wait for him, no matter how long it took.

Joel said yes—that we would do this together. We would love each other through a long-distance relationship. He promised to come back for me, for us. I held on to his promises. For ten months, we continued our long-distance relationship with ninety-two hundred miles and a twelve-hour time difference between us. We both showed interest, put in the effort, and took initiative. Where there's a will, there's a way. We communicated often and made video calls at least once a day, in addition to regular texting.

Rania joined the video calls once a week, and they began to know each other better and grew comfortable with each other. After a few months, she started calling him Papa. Joel knew that he was not going to be her stepdad, and she was not going to be his stepdaughter—it would be a father-daughter relationship. He was and is the only father she has known. She loved her papa so much, and she still does. Joel was a responsible and caring father. He still is.

I told my family about my plans. My mom was both happy and concerned for me; my dad was not as open or excited, worried about everything that could go wrong. But I knew that I was making the right decision. I wanted to do what was best and right for Rania and me. I was willing to take the risk, step out in boldness, embrace the adventure, trust God, and make decisions for myself. I knew I could trust Joel and prayerfully submitted everything to God. My parents would feel comfortable and at peace in due time; they just needed to process it all. Of course, they would have known about it sooner had they been open and understanding.

Time felt like it was moving slowly. I missed Joel so much. We did not know when we would reunite or hold each other again. I kept telling him that anything was possible and that God could turn things around, despite what was happening around the world. We should not lose hope but stay strong and optimistic. We communicated effectively about how we felt, addressing every issue that came to mind and remaining connected by making time for each other daily. We grew in love and stayed loyal to each other. I love handwritten letters, so I wrote Joel to surprise him. We also sent each other gifts every now and then.

I brought Joel, our relationship, and family before God. One day, out of the blue, I read a news article that brought joy and excitement to my heart: Singapore was opening its borders for couples who wanted to get married. I cried, knowing God had come through for me again. Joel was so happy to hear the news; and I was grateful for the faith, commitment, love, and patience he had toward me. He started organizing his work schedule and planned for his leave. Our ten months of long-distance was finally going to be over. Hurrah!

I began to complete forms and online applications. Joel arranged payments and bookings to be made for his pre-departure COVID-19 tests and the fourteen-day quarantine in Singapore. I am so grateful that he was willing to invest in me, in us. Flight tickets, quarantine hotel, and an apartment to stay in while he was in Singapore were not cheap! But Joel graciously did it for us.

I could sense God's favor upon me, and it reminded me of Ruth and Boaz from the Bible. As I loved God, kept my heart true before Him, and trusted in His sovereignty, He intervened in His perfect timing. How wonderful are God's orchestrated plans! Thank you, Jesus! I also expressed my gratitude, love, and appreciation toward Joel; and he told me I was worth it and deserved the best. I always say that I am the lucky one to have found him. He says that he is the lucky one to have found me. The truth is that we are both greatly blessed to have each other. God's hand was upon us.

Since the pandemic still raged, we had to get married at the Registry of Marriages in Singapore. Joel arrived in January 2021. He met my family, and we exchanged vows on February 5 in a small, simple ceremony with only my immediate family members present, due to health restrictions. We enjoyed a delicious, private family dinner the same evening; and then Joel remained in Singapore for one month.

He had to return to Montreal in March. Shortly after completing another fourteen-day quarantine, he started getting his apartment ready for Rania and me to arrive. He also began looking for a new and bigger apartment for us to move into as a family. He purchased flight tickets for us; I started packing and making preparations to go. I took Rania out of school and said my goodbyes to family and friends. Leaving my family was not easy, but my place was with Joel. Rania and I had a beautiful life ahead with him. God had wonderful things in store for us. He brought us together in such a beautiful, adventurous, special way.

My parents were sad to see us go and missed Rania greatly. It was a big step for Rania, too, as she had always been around my parents and younger brother. She had grown really close to them. But as sad as it was and as much as I love my country, I knew that Rania and I had to go to Montreal to begin a new chapter of our lives. My husband, her papa, waited for us excitedly. My parents were also happy for us, recognizing Joel as a good and trustworthy man. He got along well with my family. I got along well with his family, too—especially his mom, my dear mother-in-law.

Well-meaning people told me it might take a long time before we could go to Montreal, mentioning friends who were apart from their spouses for almost two years. They listed problems with immigration and other hurdles. I told myself that God was in control and had the final say. My life was in His hands. I daily brought Joel, Rania, and myself before God in prayer and trusted His will. He knew my heart, desires, and worries. He knew what was best for Joel, Rania, and me. "Trust in the Lord with all your heart; do not depend on your own understanding. Seek his will in all you do, and he will show you which path to take" (Prov. 3:5-6).

Rania and I flew to Montreal that May. Our lives are now here in Canada with Joel, and we could not be happier. God has been good and gracious to us. Through every challenge, God carries us through. His mercy endures forever. My parents visited us in August

2022, and the three of us traveled home to Singapore for five weeks that December.

I was truly happy and grateful that I could visit Pastor Chad and Jennifer in Texas again in October 2022. This time, I could introduce Joel and Rania to them in person. How wonderful! We were so refreshed, encouraged, and thankful to be able to spend time with them. It always uplifts me. I celebrated my thirty-ninth birthday there. They asked me to sing at their church, and I was honored and blessed to be there. I sang "That's the Power" by Hillsong Worship (Benjamin William Hastings). God is awesome. It is amazing how He brings people together. Joel and I are often in touch with Pastor Chad and Jennifer and are nourished by this meaningful bond we have with them. They will always have a special place in my heart.

We returned to Irving, Texas, again in March 2023 and had an amazing time. Pastor Chad and Jennifer asked me to share my testimony at their church. It was such a beautiful privilege to be able to tell my story and proclaim the goodness and love of God. Joel and I also presented a special number, "How Good the Lord Is," by Kingdom Culture Worship. Seeing God move in ways that only He can was breathtaking. The members of the church were kind and welcoming. We enjoyed every single minute of our time there. During this trip, we bonded deeper with Pastor Chad, Jennifer, and their precious family.

My parents came to see us again for three weeks that August, when we celebrated Rania's ninth birthday together. It was a wonderful time of fellowship, bonding, and reconciliation. We did many activities together, including our annual camping (glamping) again! Nature and barbecue make a nice combination! It was fun and refreshing. Rania loved every moment, spending quality time with *paati* and *thatha* (*grandmother* and *grandfather* in Tamil).

Joel was also able to have time alone with my father. They bonded further and had conversations man-to-man. My father opened up to Joel about various things and shared his own personal struggles as a man, husband, father, and grandfather. He spoke of his experiences in the army, full-time ministry, and as a missionary, mentioning his fears and uncertainties and how he had to learn to surrender it all to God. My father also talked about me and the talents God has blessed me with. Things he was not able to tell me in person, he could share with my husband.

These conversations also gave Joel an opportunity to talk about his own challenges, desires, and feelings. Joel also talked about me, our marriage, my writing, Rania, his walk with the Lord, his convictions, his journey as a father himself, and his job. They listened and learned from each other. Spending time with us brought my parents a lot of peace, and seeing us happy made them happy. They felt relieved, knowing that Rania and I were safe and well and were thankful for Joel and his kind heart. We talked about life experiences and God's faithfulness.

My parents are getting older; and seeing them brought me joy, as I have missed them. I pray that God will bless them with good health and long life and that we have many more moments together as a family. My mother's kindness, prayers, and patience and my father's generosity, jokes, and helpfulness—these gifts will never be forgotten by us. We look forward to visiting Singapore again. We are also trying for a baby now. May God's will be done in our lives. I anticipate so many great things coming. God is so good. My heart is full of hope. Love mends the gap.

As I look back on my life, I am filled with so much gratitude, appreciation, humility, and love. I am so thankful for everything God has done and is doing. Where would I be without Him? I am glad that I can include God in every aspect of my life. I am so grateful for my precious husband and daughter, whom I love with all my heart. I always say that Joel and I are two halves of the same heart, and Rania is my heart in human form. I am so grateful to be Rania's mommy. She is an amazing daughter, and I love her with every inch of my being.

Life is such a beautiful journey with so many lessons and blessings along the way. We worship an interpersonal God. He cares about every aspect of your life. Involve Him in everything. Life is better with Jesus.

Yes, challenges, struggles, and frustrations come; but I am daily learning to do better and growing as a person, child of God, wife, and mother. I am learning to constantly honor God, my husband, and daughter and to show grace toward my parents and family members. I am learning to practice self-control and patience. Mindfulness, self-awareness, daily reflection, and the help of the Holy Spirit are needed.

I sometimes see irritability, anger, rage, harsh parenting, insecurity, fear, jealousy, and anxiety subtly showing up in me. The years of abuse, assault, betrayal, and neglect have symptoms that follow. Some could be caused by hormones, age, and other factors; but I am learning to practice self-compassion and not be too hard on myself. I am learning to show grace to others around me and to lean into God more and be open before Him. I am learning to discuss my emotions with my spouse and connect with him in love, intimacy, and prayer. I am learning to bring it all to God, to lay it all at His feet.

I am learning to make time for God daily and to come before God together as a couple and family, to get help when necessary, including therapy, if needed. I am learning to confide in trusted, godly, sisters in Christ—women who can pray for me and with me and with whom I can build a solid friendship, women I can uplift and edify as "iron sharpens iron" (Prov. 27:17).

I am learning to recognize my triggers and find ways to manage them and to tame my tongue without always having the last say. God is my Defense and Tower of Refuge, and I trust Him every single day of my life. I am learning to love and appreciate my husband deeply and to be transparent with him while learning to love myself and embrace my body. I am learning to be patient, gentle, kind, and gracious toward my daughter and not pass down any brokenness to her. I am learning to cherish every single moment and count my blessings. I am learning to release my grip on things and to be a prayerful wife and mother.

Most importantly, I am learning that God is not done with me. He is faithful to carry me through every stage and season of life. He is a God Who heals, restores, gently chastises, cares, delivers, and loves me. I am truly happy, thankful, and at peace. I love this life that God has blessed me with, and I do not want to take it for granted. The love of Jesus has made my life worth living. I am in a much better place in life right now. I feel whole and complete. My heart is filled with thanksgiving; and when challenging days come, I turn to my Fortress, Deliverer, Rock, Strength, Shield, Stronghold, and the Horn of my Salvation: Jesus.

Remember, your story isn't over yet! God can and will turn things around for you. Jesus wants to take you by the hand and go through daily life with you. Reach out to Him and never let go. You are loved!

"And I am certain that God, who began the good work within you, will continue his work until it is finally finished on the day when Christ Jesus returns" (Phil. 1:6).

Bibliography

AZ Quotes. "Grace Allen Quotes." Accessed June 27, 2024, https://www.azquotes.com/author/265-Gracie_Allen.

Bregel, Sarah. "Not Every Mother Feels Like a Natural Mom—And That's OK." Calm.com. Accessed June 27, 2024. https://calm4kids.org/not every mother feels like a natural mom and thats ok.

Chambers, Gary D. *The Five Love Languages: How to Express Heartfelt Commitment to Your Mate.* Nashville: Lifeway Press, 2010.

Quotesndnotes. "Quotes 'nd Notes." Accessed November 5, 2024. Quotes and Notes. https://quotesndnotes.tumblr.com/post/182484246946/sometimes-home-isnt-4-walls-its-2-eyes-and-a.

About the Author

Grace Valentine is an old soul who wears her heart on her sleeve. A living testimony of God's mercy and goodness, she loves to sing, play hand drums, write, talk, and make a difference. Born and raised in Singapore, she lived as a missionary in Uganda for two years; moved to the United Arab Emirates for seven years—during which time she traveled the world as a flight attendant—and now lives in Canada with her beautiful family—loving Jesus, empowering others, and touching lives one day at a time!

Ambassador International's mission is to magnify the Lord Jesus Christ and promote His Gospel through the written word.

We believe through the publication of Christian literature, Jesus Christ and His Word will be exalted, believers will be strengthened in their walk with Him, and the lost will be directed to Jesus Christ as the only way of salvation.

For more information about
AMBASSADOR INTERNATIONAL
please visit:

www.ambassador-international.com
@AmbassadorIntl
www.facebook.com/AmbassadorIntl

Ambassador International
GREENVILLE, SOUTH CAROLINA & BELFAST, NORTHERN IRELAND

www.ambassador-international.com
Magnifying Jesus while promoting His gospel through the written word.

Thank you for reading this book!

You make it possible for us to fulfill our mission, and we are grateful for your partnership.

To help further our mission, please consider leaving us a review on your social media, favorite retailer's website, Goodreads or Bookbub, or our website, and check out some of our other books on the next page!

More from Ambassador International

Growing up in small-town Ohio, Jill van Opstal-Popa never dreamed she would be making her home among the orphaned children of Brazil. But when she and her husband set out to be missionaries, they found themselves building a home for the children who had no home. From the heart of a mother to many comes the stories of the people of Brazil. Your heart will be pulled to the stories of each child whose story is unique but also like so many others.

Take some deep breaths with Bonica Brown, who has found what her soul has been thirsting for in God's Word and in the gift of His roses and honeysuckle. If you have ever needed a friend to walk through the ups and downs of motherhood with you, Bonica is waiting for you to introduce you to her very Best Friend, Jesus Christ.

Throughout her years serving alongside her husband, who pastored Southside Baptist Church (now Fellowship Greenville) in Greenville, South Carolina, for over thirty years, Elizabeth Rice Handford has had the opportunity to touch many lives with her daily devotionals. In her new devotional, take a dive into one hundred of Libby's devotionals, compiled from a look back through her writings and life experiences.

www.ingramcontent.com/pod-product-compliance
Lightning Source LLC
Chambersburg PA
CBHW070451090426
42735CB00012B/2510